Story-Based Selling

Story-Based Selling

Create, Connect, and Close

Jeff Bloomfield

AP Axon Publishing

This edition published by Axon Publishing, LLC|8469 Mason Montgomery Road, Suite 3|Mason, Ohio 45040

First Edition

ISBN: 978-1-7337870-0-0

Library of Congress Cataloging-in-Publication Data
Bloomfield, Jeff.
 Story-Based Selling: Create, Connect, and Close / Jeff Bloomfield. --
Third edition. p149 cm6x9
 Includes bibliographical references.
 Summary: "Founder of sales training and development organization presents his theories about storytelling that he believes to be the most powerful way to connect to feelings of trust in others. He teaches techniques, based on neuroscience studies of communication, to create engaging stories that breakdown barriers of mistrust and enable productive interactions with customers."-- Provided by publisher.
 ISBN ISBN: 978-1-7337870-0-0 (hardbound book: alk. paper)
 1. Selling--Psychological aspects. 2. Storytelling--Psychological aspects. 3. Interpersonal communication. I. Title.
 HF5438.8.P75B56 2014 658.85--dc23

                    2013041869

Interior book design and production by Janice Benight

Manufactured in the United States of America
10 9 8 7 6 5 4 3

To my beautiful, supportive, intelligent wife, Hazel. Thank you for your constant gift of patience, love, and forgiveness. You are the embodiment of faith, hope, and love. To my amazingly gifted dancer, musician, and people magnet, Gracie. You constantly remind me of all that's good in this world. You are a bright shining light. To my inventive, creative, brilliant son, Drew. When the teleporter is ready, I'll go first! You are going to change the world. You three are the source of my greatest joy, and I'm humbled to be part of your stories.

And finally to Papaw. You planted the seeds of story in my soul, and I hope you're looking down with that famous smile, watching them grow.

Contents

Acknowledgments

They say it takes a village to raise a child. It also takes one to write a book! Especially when the author is, at times, the village idiot . . . There are many folks who have had a hand in this book coming to life. First, to all my clients over the past few years who have walked the Story-Based Journey with me. Thank you for taking a risk to try something a little out of your comfort zone! A special thanks to Kim, Heather, Dominic, Matt, Chris, Steve, Mark, Bill, Mike, John and Joe for having the vision to take this program into your larger organizations. And thank you for the laughter, tears and friendship we share at every session.

To Ford, thank you for your mentorship and friendship. Transformational Leadership is changing the world! To Larry, thank you for getting me out of the "author" starting blocks and headed in the right direction. Steve, thank you for your trust and friendship. Greg, thank you for pulling me up by my bootstraps, smacking me around a little bit and forcing me to get this program officially into a book!

To my parents, Roger & Linda, thank you for your years of support and encouragement. To my little sister, Alisha, and brother, Brad, thank you for all the ammunition you've provided me for my stories over the years! I love you all very much.

Finally, to my Grandmother, Mary. You are the matriarch of all matriarchs and I pray that my story turns out half as well as yours.

Introduction

Who doesn't love a good story? From the youngest child to the most cynical adult, everyone has that tale that speaks to them. Their grandest hopes, their worst fears, their deepest loves, and, yes, their darkest anger are all on display in that one special revealing chronicle. I can remember as a child dreading going to the doctor's office, while at the same time excited to pick up the latest addition of *Highlights Magazine*, which always featured stories of adventure, fantasy, and morality, with recurring stories about such unique and captivating figures as Baba Yaga, the Russian witch, whose cauldron sat atop two live chicken legs.

And for some of us over the age of forty we likely remember receiving our first Luke Skywalker light saber from the epic space odyssey *Star Wars*, and convincing our dad or brother to pick up the used gift wrapping paper roll and battling us for supremacy of the universe. Most of us have probably even committed many lines to memory ("Luke . . . I'm you're father"). Those over twenty grew up on adventure series like *Harry Potter*, *The Chronicles of Narnia*, and *The Lord of the Rings* trilogy.

The point? Stories are effective. They work. Stories *influence* us. They influence us because they lead to a point, because they bring someone to a realization. The greatest compliment you can give an author is to call him a great storyteller. With Mark Twain, writing was his craft, story was the art. Sometimes it's about good and evil, and sometimes, as with almost every joke, it's simply a laugh. How many jokes do you know that begin "A guy walks into a bar?" And how many of us remember crawling onto the lap of a parent or grandparent to hear stories that began "Once upon a time . . .?" If you have young children of your own, you are likely doing this same exercise nightly.

Our greatest historians, our most memorable writers, and our most influential religious figures all used stories to explain their principles. Jesus could have said, as did the Ten Commandments, "Thou shalt not..." but instead, He chose "A certain man went down from Jerusalem to Jericho . . ."[1] In fact, the entire Bible is full of illustrations, (parables) analogies, and metaphors. If the creator of the universe chose to communicate in story form, that's good enough for me!

Even though few people have read it cover to cover, everyone knows the story of Moby Dick, the great white whale. And some of our most famous stories may not have ever occurred—yet they so perfectly capture truths that endure. (Think of George Washington and the cherry tree). Did Abraham Lincoln actually read pages of a book at the end of each row he plowed? The story makes it seem so, but to my knowledge, no credible clip has been posted to You Tube. The point is, from Thucydides to Tolstoy, from Herodotus to Hemingway, people have known even before the written word that the best way to explain something is through a story.

Truth is revealed in stories, fictitious or real, because this connects with an audience. A character will always deliver a greater impact than a pie chart.

"We are our stories. We compress years of experience, view, and emotion into a few compact narratives that we convey to others and tell to ourselves."
—DANIEL PINK, *A Whole New Mind*

The purpose of this book is to show you how you can use a story-based approach to improve how you communicate and ultimately improve the way you *influence* others, not for control or manipulation but for mutual benefit. Companies of all sizes and shapes are using this program to improve sales effectiveness, but the underlying principles and science behind the program teach effective "communication" in both business and personal situations. Sales is merely one category of communication to greatly benefit from these concepts. Regardless of your position or title, this program will most assuredly change the way you communicate forever.

Often "sales" gets a stereotypical bad rap. Just the mere mention of the word "salesperson" conjures images of manipulative used-car salesmen or that whacky Sham-Wow guy from the infomercial ready to take advantage of us and steal our money. Sure, those people are out there, but, as we are well aware, there are some unsavory doctors, lawyers, movie stars, and politicians too.

The reality is, and I love to debate this with anyone who disagrees . . . we are *all* salespeople. WHAT?!? Yep. We are all salespeople. Think about it for just a second. "Sales" is more than pushing a product or service. It is concentrated, intentional influence. We have simply confined the "business" version of this to "sales." Remember when you recently tried to convince your four-year-old to eat his or her peas? Remember when your doctor recently tried to convince you to change your eating habits and get some exercise? How about your pastor last Sunday explaining how you may want to re-think where you spend your time and resources? And this goes on and on. All day, every day, we try to influence someone, and we are generally under the spell of someone else's influence.

In our live workshops, I challenge participants to think of a time when they were speaking to someone else—anyone else—and they were *not* trying to influence them to one end or another. Stop and think about it for a second. What were you actually trying to accomplish with speaking? Even when we think we are simply sharing stories to be funny or participating in a friend-to-friend discussion, influence is still in play. You are either subconsciously trying to make them like you, or possibly trying to convince them of thinking about something differently, but the point is, you are *still* trying to influence. Scary, huh? You can try to justify some rationalization that makes you believe this is not true if you'd like, but the reality is, it's true. In fact, no one has ever been able to give me an example where this is not the case.

Once we accept that we are all selling something, we can get over the hurdle of change and begin to really focus on the skills that will make us better at communication—and better at having influence and better at selling. This book and program will equip you with the tools and steps to understand how "storytelling" coupled with the latest neuroscience can make you an incredibly powerful "influencer." When it comes to influencing others, you can do it from a place of power and manipulation (we think of Hitler, as well as many politicians) or you can choose to operate from a place of *mutual benefit*. When you begin to use these tools with a guided purpose of mutual benefit, you will see tremendous, lasting results.

In the beginning . . .

My introduction to this "story-based communication" concept came from my grandfather, known to others as "Willie," but just "Papaw" to me. He lived on the opposite end of my family's one hundred-acre farm in central Ohio. It was just about a fifty-yard walk for me to drop by after school for a snack. Just as often, however, I would get a story from Papaw. Although he had only an eighth grade education and worked in a steel mill, he had abundant wisdom. He knew people. He knew life. Once when my father was struggling with his grades, Papaw instructed him to dig a knee-deep ditch from our house to the barn—about three hundred feet. It took dad all summer, and he worked hard.

When he finished, he looked to Papaw who approved, but then said, "Now, fill it back in!"

My father was stunned. "Why in the world did you have me spend the entire summer digging a ditch you don't need?"

My grandpa replied, "Did you enjoy spending all summer digging that ditch, son?"

"Of course not!"

Grandpa then said, "The world needs ditch diggers, too. Unless you want to be one of them, get your grades up and get an education."

Message received. Dad's grades dramatically improved. He could have just shown my father a graph of what college graduates make versus those who do not finish high school, but how long would that resonate? He gave my father a story, but left the ending up to him.

Papaw constantly used some form of a story-based approach to everything he taught me. One time, he taught a friend and me a dramatic lesson on the scientific power of electrical conductivity.

We had just heard about a guy getting electrocuted while standing in a pool of water. I asked Papaw how this great mystery was possible. He simply said "conductivity, son."

Huh? we thought. That famous grin appeared on his face as he gave us both a freshly opened bottle of Coke to sip on while we walked with him. I wasn't sure where we were headed, but I knew there would be a lesson involved.

When we got to the edge of the farm where the fence ran, he looked over and said, "You boys about done with those Cokes?"

"Yep," we replied.

"I'm sure you've got to take a bathroom pit-stop, so go ahead and do it over there in the weeds. Make sure you shoot for the electric fence while you're doing it."

As you might have guessed, two nine-year-old boys quickly learned how electricity travels through a liquid. I can still hear his laughter bellowing through the field.

Sometimes the truth hurts.

* * *

I didn't realize it then, but the *way* he communicated was intentional. He knew how to connect with others—through illustrations, analogies, and metaphors. He was an amazing teacher.

Just before my twelfth birthday, I jumped off the bus at the end of Papaw's driveway and began to make that fifty-yard walk to his house. I could almost taste my Grandma's biscuits and gravy, and I wondered what lesson Papaw would have in store for me as well.

Normally the only vehicle in their driveway was Papaw's green Chevy pick-up truck. Strangely, on this day there were several cars as well. As I got closer to the house, my dad met me on the porch and sent me to the woods to clean up what was left from our old rusty red firewood cart that had toppled over in the creek the day before. I still didn't have a clue as to what was going on. When I heard the ambulance come screaming down our old dirt road, I started to get the picture that something was wrong.

I never got to see my Papaw again. As the ambulance sped away, he slipped into a coma and never returned. He had stage-four lung cancer and only a few people knew this, and one who didn't know was his towheaded favorite grandson.

When Papaw died, I lost my best friend, but his stories and lessons stay with me. The legacy he left me was a foundation that I will never forget and now helps a new generation of storytellers influence their children and grandchildren.

As I went through college, I became a storyteller myself. Although I didn't realize it at the time, what made my stories successful in business were the intangibles he taught me. I communicated with people through stories, using analogies, metaphors, and personal illustrations just as he had. Eventually, I found myself in the biotech field, where I had the privilege of launching two revolutionary molecules to help treat—of all things—lung cancer. During that time, I sold with passion. I sold with purpose. I sold our drugs because I knew what one more year, one more month, or even one more day of life meant to the families of those with lung cancer. It meant they might just have a little more time, more moments with the people they loved. Perhaps a graduation, a birth, a wedding. Maybe even just one more story from their Papaw.

Over time, I came to notice that my approach to sales differed a great deal from my peers. They used clinical data, facts, and statistics, but I used . . . you guessed it—stories. I found the story behind the patients. What were their hopes, their dreams? What did they want to see the treatment accomplish? How could I be their advocate? This approach ran counter to much of what was prevalent in sales and sales training at that time. We had been taught to uncover "pain" and "problems," to essentially probe our potential customers into submission until we found a "solution." Yet when I shared my story-based approach with others, they too saw instant results.

**"I realized the importance of having a story today
is what really separates companies. People don't just
wear our shoes, they tell our story."**
—BLAKE MYCOSKIE, CEO, Tom's Shoes

Off the top of your head, can you tell me the most interesting PowerPoint presentation you have ever seen? How about the most compelling spreadsheet? Even a bad story is likely to make a more significant impact on any audience than a steady diet of facts and figures. Think about yourself as an audience first. What would you want?

It's pretty obvious, after all: People buy from people they *trust*. People trust those they *like*, and people like those they *connect* with. Most will tell you trust comes from the gut; it's instinctive. It's as if we are genetically pre-programmed to seek out relationships built on trust. Because we are.

I learned this in the biotech industry, scouring neuroscience articles. Yet trust, and how to communicate through trust, is not something generally taught in schools, universities, or even in training rooms in today's corporate America. Here's the thing: we don't need to create programs that attempt to show people how to build trust.

We need to show people how to connect! Once you connect, you are more likeable. When you are likeable, you are inherently more trustworthy.

The intent of *Story-Based Selling* is not to introduce a brand-new "sales training de jour" to you or your organization. You've made it this far because you've worked and trained hard and you know what you are doing. Think of it this way. You've built a pretty durable, sleek sports car and you know how to drive. This program doesn't replace your car or its engine. It merely provides a new type of "rocket fuel" to enable you to drive farther, faster, and win more races.

What I intend to show you is how to leverage the way the brain processes information through stories to establish a foundation of trust. Decision-making will follow. Here are just a few of the things I hope to share with you about the power of communicating through stories (and also about the science and research supporting this concept):

- Sales is merely a form of communication, which itself is a form of influencing the decisions of others. We want to pursue influence that is "mutually beneficial" as opposed to controlling and manipulative.

- People buy from people they trust. They trust people they like and they like people they connect with. This program will teach you how communication, when done correctly, leads to favorable decisions, and this occurs from making an emotional connection, not using logical arguments.

- We train people incorrectly—especially those in sales— to sell features, facts, and statistics. These all appeal to logic and are interpreted by a part of the brain that drives skepticism. This approach often leads to lack of trust or even apprehension.

- The use of stories, analogies, metaphors, and visuals—when used effectively—can drive the listener to the area of the brain that makes an emotional connection and drives results towards a positive decision.

- When you build your story-based foundation on humility, vulnerability, and authenticity you accelerate the emotional connection and subsequent associated trust.

- Anyone can build a portfolio of stories with the right training—which this book provides—but you need to adopt the right *attitude*. When we are open to something new and different, we naturally allow ourselves a greater capacity to improve.

As we examine these dynamics, I will show you how our society and educational system has trained you to be "left brained," and why some people are great communicators and others are . . . not so much. And I will show how the incorporation of stories, told with humility and authenticity, will revolutionize your sales, your performance, and your organization.

Story-Based Selling

1

The Evolution of Communication

"Do You understand the words
that are coming out of my mouth?"

—Detective Carter, *Rush Hour*

In order to see a path forward to an improved, story-based communication "style" we must first understand how we've arrived at our current destination of communication. There are so many variables to our communication approach today that have been impacted, both directly and indirectly, from our generational predecessors.

From this background we can comprehend how we've unintentionally developed into a transactional, unemotional, disconnected society. As you might have guessed, this is in complete contradiction to our desire for relational, emotional connections with our customers. Understanding this evolution will illuminate our path, allowing us to "stem the tide" of this unproductive style and develop a more effective, relational, story-based approach to communication.

In today's society, it is virtually impossible to talk about connections without touching on the rise of social media. Most notable on the list is, of course, Facebook. In 2012 Facebook.com was the most visited site on the World Wide Web. Every day millions of people go there, but what are they looking for? Quite simply, they are looking for a

> "It is true that storytelling reveals meaning without committing the error of defining it ..."
>
> —Hannah Arendt
> German political philosopher,
> *"Isak Dinesen: 1885-1963"*

1

connection. They want to feel a part of what their friends, family, and co-workers are doing by adding a comment or "liking" a photo or status.

But what is the drawback? We can very easily substitute a surface-level online world for real life. Just because someone has over one thousand friends on Facebook does not mean the person has that many true connections. Somewhere over the countless hours spent in front of the screen, that line has been blurred. Real human interaction can seem like a lost art.

This is certainly not an indictment against any of these sites. In fact, they can be a good thing, and an effective tool, but it is never a substitute for getting to know someone. Just remember, you are more than a status update. You have a story to tell. So, how did we get from sittin' around the campfire to sittin' around the MacBook, anyway?

Yakety Yak

To say that communication skills have undergone a revolution in the past twenty years is like saying Mel Gibson occasionally puts his foot in his mouth. The rise of cell phones, and particularly texting, has revolutionized the way people "talk," literally to the point of changing the spelling of words ("u" for "you," "lol" for "laughing out loud," and so on). While most business people do not communicate primarily through texting, instant access communication has changed our speech and writing habits.

For one thing, the cell phone revolution has placed a premium on brevity, especially when it comes to texting. People simply don't write long texts. Twitter is even more restrictive, forcing you to state your point in no more than one hundred forty characters.

> "If you would not be forgotten
> As soon as you are dead and rotten
> Either write things worth reading
> Or do things worth the writing."
> —saying attributed to BENJAMIN FRANKLIN

This tends to produce some extremely pithy and clever posts. It also, however, destroys the entire concept of a point supported by an effective narrative. But the biggest casualty of this revolution is the story. Who has time for writing a story requiring one hundred forty characters or a twenty-word text message?

"You must un-learn what you have learned."

Remember the classic character Yoda in the *Star Wars* series? Introduced for the first time in *The Empire Strikes Back,* Yoda was known for his brilliant wisdom doled out in sentences that were structurally backward. Such "Strong you must be" and "To Tatooine you must go.") While instructing Luke Skywalker in using the "Force," at one point a frustrated Yoda insists "You must un-learn what you have learned." This is pretty insightful. Whether it's a bad golf swing or a flawed business procedure, the first step toward success is to modify your behavior. In many cases, that requires you to go back to the basics and start afresh.

I took a golf lesson once and the instructor told me at the very first lesson, "Prepare yourself. You will actually become worse at golf before you get better. We have to un-do the bad swing habits you've developed on your own." When you are a bad golfer to begin with, it's certainly not pleasing to think that you'll have to get even *worse* before you get better! For most of you, you are already fairly good communicators or you wouldn't have made it this far! I will, however, be asking you to take a few "golf lessons" along the way.

**"The stories of past courage can define that ingredient—
they can teach, they can offer hope, they can provide inspiration."**
—JOHN F. KENNEDY, *Profiles in Courage*

How have you been trained to communicate? Traditionally, especially in business settings, the emphasis is on delivering information clearly, concisely, and most of all, briefly. Indeed, we call meetings where one person provides information to others "a briefing." In our modern business society, more often than not this involves the Microsoft PowerPoint presentation, where "bullet points" are presented with short summations of longer (but only slightly longer) points the speaker will make. In theory, the recipient of the information should be able to take home the "bullet points" and have the information needed to make a decision.

Every organization in the history of sales has been trained in a certain approach. This is normal. Most of this can be traced back to how the individuals in the organization were educated, and this means we must look at the story of education in America.

Production Line Education

Our country's founders created the American education system as a means to prepare people (at the time, only boys) to assume the duties of leadership in America by training them in mathematics, grammar, a patriotic history, and religion. George Washington wrote to George Chapman in 1784, admonishing, "The best means of forming a manly, virtuous and happy people, will be found in the right education of youth."

Most Americans learned, or were taught, through stories—stories told by their parents, their ministers, their neighbors, and often, most exciting of all, by the itinerant traveler from afar who would tell wild tales of fierce Indians, exotic animals, or exciting adventures. The early books in the one-room schools were also story-based, from the McGuffey Readers to, as late as the 1950s, the Dick and Jane books.

Impactful anecdotes, genealogies, family and national histories, and even recipes were passed down through stories, which is why they often were not even written down. Morality was handed down through stories about John Henry (that man, even in his frailty, is superior to the finest machine because he has a soul); or the Wizard of Oz (that there is hope in the direst of situations); or Johnny Appleseed (that the tiniest effort can result in mighty results).

As the United States became an industrial nation between 1800 and 1840, schools were democratized and secularized. States began to extend education to the modern-day 8th grade, but the curriculum was still told through stories. But not for long.

After the Civil War the titans of industry saw the need for more skill-based learning in their labor force, and this is where we see a transition from the one-room schoolhouse to the larger, more centralized, government-regulated education systems.

When Eli Whitney took on his first contract to make muskets for the U.S. Army, he tried to recruit top-flight gunsmiths. But they were expensive, and it could take a skilled craftsman a month to make a single musket. Whitney didn't have the luxury of time. He was among the first to organize an assembly-line process with gun-making machines at various stations, and he found that an unskilled worker could be trained quickly for a single task.

> "Better spend an extra hundred or two on your son's education, than leave it to him in your will."
> —GEORGE ELIOT
> *The Mill on the Floss*

It didn't take long for American schools to begin to resemble a factory assembly line where the work done in one department (the course) was the same every year. There was little collaboration between one department and the next while the product (the student) was processed in batches (by year of birth) and the completed product (graduates) were all out of the same mold.

They were measured by their ability to memorize and regurgitate information. Little to no application or creative thinking was needed. Now, if you have children, think of their educational environment. They start out in pre-school with kids all the same age, given all the same learning material that's age-appropriate as dictated by whom? Then, they proceed through elementary school with the same kids grouped by age and force-fed a steady diet of memorization and regurgitation of factual information. Does it ever change all the way through elementary and high school? Through college?

Given this structure, can you see why creativity and innovation would be difficult to accept—let alone initiate? Teachers, handed the workflow and schedule (curriculum) by the plant managers (school boards and politicians), have little flexibility or authority to change, especially when since the 20th century they were supervised by a union, a foreman (the union leader), and paid and protected by seniority (tenure). Yet in the process, the "system" lost sight of the goal: to prepare people to have productive jobs to meet the needs of the times and the economy of the future. In many ways, today we have traded the art and effectiveness of story telling for the expediency of a production-line education.

The American education system is ready for a new focus. Not in recent memory have the stars aligned as they are now, with the clamor for innovation and the ability to develop and use new technologies greater than ever. Both sides of the American political debate agree that the United States needs to replace the jobs lost from the industrial-era workforce, and that we bring our children up to speed with the competitive educational systems of other countries.

Part of this demand is that we refocus the system to teach innovation, not just facts. These "facts" are becoming increasingly less important than the skills and abilities to find solutions. Students may not know the capital of Belarus, but must understand the process to find it. And to "teach" creativity and innovation we need to employ the whole brain, which we will delve into more deeply in the next chapter.

You've Gotta Read if You Wanna Lead

I once heard the head of a large organization say, "If you don't read, you can't lead." There is much to that. How can you develop a good vocabulary, smooth phrasing, and appropriate illustrations, analogies, and metaphors if you are not well read? Certainly reading for enjoyment is useful by itself, but try this: the next time you read a book—even a thriller or romance—when you see a phrase that catches your eye, or dialogue that seems especially clever, make a note of it. Try to lock that away for future use.

Great speakers and communicators are not born. They practice and study. Abraham Lincoln read all sorts of books, including fables, the Bible, and even boring, transactional law books. When it came time for him to step up on a stump and make a speech, the words that came out were not all his, but rather many were phrases he had absorbed by his *reading* ("a house divided against itself cannot stand" for example is straight from the Bible).

Many times when people start developing their story, they will try to impress their audience with a little pepper, or as I refer to it, *artificial flavoring*. This is not necessary, nor is it advised, as authenticity is paramount. The more you read, and the more you listen, you will discover how words are used by great communicators. Over time, you will have a deep pool of exceptional resources from which you can pull your stories. But remember, it is not just great words that elicit a great response; it is the storyteller's passion behind them that makes the ordinary suddenly extraordinary.

But I would take this breadth of experience beyond reading. In our modern world, with so much of our communication done through television, movies, music, and the Internet, it is essential—no matter how much some of it may turn you off—that you have a familiarity with pop culture. Almost everyone else will, so you'll need these examples.

Movie references to *Ben-Hur* or *Gone with the Wind* and musical references to the Beatles are so outdated as to often cause listeners to mumble "who?" and "what?" If you don't know what an iPad does, or what Lady Gaga and Adele are known for (and even, perhaps, by the time of this publication these names and phrases will be "old news"), it will be hard for you to communicate with some of your target audience.

But these are tactics supporting a larger strategy. The goal here is to re-train you to be an effective communicator using stories. And to do that, we must employ all your brain, not just half of it! Let's take a look at how some of our best-known leaders have done this over time.

How Great Leaders Communicate

Before we move on from the "evolution of communication" and into the science behind how we make decisions and process information, we should take a peek at who, in our line of great communicators, have instinctively bucked this transactional process and found ways to connect in spite of their training.

What makes a great leader? According to best-selling author Stephen R. Covey, "Leadership is communicating to people their worth and potential so clearly that they are inspired to *see* it in themselves." He goes on to argue that leaders (1) inspire trust, (2) clarify purpose, (3) align systems so that there is no internal conflict, and (4) unleash talent.[2]

How has this actually played out with communicators throughout history? How many people realized you could teach how to be an effective communicator? Trust is formed in right brain, and at an emotional level (more on this in the next chapter). Going back to Covey's description, then, one could say that a great leader is someone who inspires others to act on the basis of mutual benefit through the emotional connection of trust. Important historical figures who have led movements have not always been "great leaders," but rather have motivated out of fear and manipulation, not out of mutual benefit and trust through an emotional connection.[3] The best, however, took a different approach.

Consider, for example, Abraham Lincoln, who appealed to Americans at the end of a bloody war with the following words at the end of his Second Inaugural Address on March 4, 1865:

> With malice toward none, with charity for all, with firmness in the right as God gives us to see the right, let us strive on to finish the work we are in, to bind up the nation's wounds, to care for him who shall have borne the battle and for his widow and his orphan, to do all which may achieve and cherish a just and lasting peace among ourselves and with all nations.

Lincoln knew that hope and dreams of a better future invoke our emotions, and lasted longer than hatred and anger.

Now lets look at a modern-day example of someone who connects with people: television producer and host Oprah Winfrey. The most important thing Oprah does is to lay her vulnerability out for all the audience to see. She is genuine and authentic, and her emotions come with the package. This connects with people. When someone characterized Oprah's success as "Oprah cries," it wasn't far from the truth. When delivering a commencement address to Howard University in 2007, Oprah said:

> I spent eight years in Baltimore. I knew in those years in Baltimore that I was unhappy being a television news reporter. But the voice of my father . . . said don't you give up that job, girl. You're never going to make $25,000 in one year. That's my father's dream for me. But God could dream a bigger dream than you can dream for yourself. And so I tried to live in the space of God's dream. And the television executives told me when I was in Baltimore that I was just—it was too much. I was too big, and I was too black. They told me that I was too engaged, that I was too emotional, I was too-too much for the news and so they put me on a talk show one day just to run out my contract. And that was the beginning of my story.[4]

The great evangelist Billy Graham exhibited a down-home authenticity that would cause millions of people to fill stadiums to listen to his sermons. It did not matter if they were truly attracted by his message, his genuineness made them open to hearing it. Even if a person left a Billy Graham Crusade without accepting Graham's Christian message, few walked out without thinking he was speaking to them *individually.*

> I'm encouraged to believe that Americans at this hour are striving to retain their spiritual identity. . . . [Some time

ago there was] a picture of Betsy Ross sewing the first American flag and over the picture was the caption, 'Time to check our stitches!' Let's check the stitches of racism that still exists in America. . . . Let's check the stitches of foreign policy to be sure that our goals and objectives are in keeping with the American dream . . .[5]

Do you notice something about those great speakers who were, or are, truly "great" people? They all speak to dreams and aspirations, not fear or anger. They also consistently speak in stories, analogies, and metaphors.

All successful people are not necessarily great communicators or even effective leaders. Steve Jobs—a great innovator, brilliant conceptualizer—was terrific when it came to communicating about technology and "stuff," but when it came to motivating people, he left a lot to be desired. Driven and trending toward "my way or the highway," Jobs certainly did not inspire through emotional attachment or connection. I guess there isn't an "app" for everything.

I have reviewed countless lists of the qualities of top communicators and even developed a few of my own over the years, but Nathan Hurst, a pastor in Cranberry Township, Pa. has, in my opinion nailed it with the following "Characteristics of a great communicator":[6]

Content: You can't substitute "Style" for substance. Every great communicator has had something of value to say. They champion a cause.

Passion: People matter. To Great communicators, people matter greatly. It's easy to love to speak to people but do you love the people you speak to?

Credibility: Truly great communicators are so because they "practice what they preach." The scriptures are true, "your sin will find you out." Once credibility is gone almost all influence is gone with it.

Preparedness: Great communicators can but rarely, if ever "wing it." Consistent study makes for ever-ready preparedness.

Note-free: Great communicators speak from the heart, not a notebook. Breaking from predetermined notes and speaking with conviction to compel the audience to join in, is a hallmark of a great communicator.

Brevity: Great communicators are able to take complex information and condense it to a riveting thirty-minute message. Most long-winded messages are attempts to inform, not to connect.

Conviction: Great communicators give more than a simple message; they give an impassioned invitation to participate.

Self-revealing: Great communicators are real with their listeners. They avoid ego filled, self-absorbed statements and share real life struggles, only after they have conquered a challenge. Great communicators are not looking for sympathy or acceptance but rather hope that their struggles may benefit others.

Confidence: Confidence is not the absence of fear but moving forward in-spite of it.

Tone: Great communicators know their audience is listening to every breath. They make every syllable count.

Story-telling: All of history's great communicators can tell amazing stories. Fact or fiction has little to do with this ability.

Props: Most great communicators use props. While in the moment, a microphone stand can represent anything from a fireman's pole to a golf club. This type of creativity seems to be very spontaneous.

Humor: All great communicators have a well-developed sense of humor, and it shows. Great communicators build on moments of hilarity that doesn't lose their audience.

Pause: Great communicators pause in order for their audience to digest the given information.

Eye Contact: Great communicators make eye contact. Each person in the audience feels that the speaker is looking right at them.

Intensity: Great communicators deliver a message with intensity. Volume and speed have little to do with intensity. When the heart has conviction, intensity is the aftermath.

Movement: Great communicators know 55 percent of what they say is interpreted through body movement. Great communicators speak more with their body than their words.

Decision: A great communicator will demand a response from the hearer. Under their influence people are compelled to change. A call is made for a specific and personal decision.

Where do you fit in? As salespeople, you have a particular style, and your customers perceive you in a specific way. The majority of what is happening is on the subconscious level, but you can't improve what you don't understand. So let's shift our attention to the science behind successful communication. Once we fully understand how the brain processes information, develops trust, and makes decisions, we can begin to tap into that incredible super-computer to *intentionally* craft our communication to maximize the brain's inherent system.

WHAT'S *YOUR* STORY?

❋ *Who do you know that's a great communicator? Why?*

❋ *Where did you develop your communication style?*

❋ *How has our current educational system influenced your communication style?*

❋ *How much do you read on a monthly basis?*

❋ *What qualities in your communication style do you feel need the most improvement?*

2

The Science Behind the Story

"Weird Science"
by Oingo Boingo, 1985

The Emancipation of Interpretation

We begin our journey down neuroscience lane by uncovering how we interpret and retain information. There are scores of confirmatory research studies—some done very recently in fact—that guide us specifically towards a story-based communication approach as the most effective way to make an impact. In a recent study by the London Business School, they demonstrated the following retention rates:[7]

When the presenter used:
- Statistics/facts only   **5-10%** retention
- Statistics combined with stories/visuals   **25-30%** retention
- Storytelling alone   **65-70%** retention

That's a potential 65% increase in retention when using storytelling as a stand-alone communication style versus facts alone. Think about your last sales appointment. How much of it was driven by facts and statistics? Now you know the customer remembered 5% of what you said!

In a related study, researchers from Princeton University found that the brains of speakers and listeners can become synchronized as they converse, and that this "neural coupling" is the key to effective communication.[8] Partners began to unconsciously imitate each other and to adopt similar grammatical structures, mirror body postures, and synchronize speaking rates. Through functional MRI, they determined that not only did their brains synchronize when using a visual communication approach, but the listener's brain also lit up in the exact same portion of the brain as the speaker. Now, that's what I call a connection!

We also know from the National Training Laboratory at the World Bank the amount that we remember from the following:[9]

- lectures about the subject   5%

- reading about the subject   10%

- audio visual aids   20%

- demonstration of the material   30%

- discussion about the material   50%

- practice   75%

- teaching others about the material   90%

As Confucius said nearly 2,500 years ago:

I hear and I forget. **(5%)**

I see and I remember. **(10-30%)**

I do and I understand. **(50-90%)**

When it comes to connecting, we all possess types of "mirror" neurons that subconsciously allow people to establish a common ground during conversations—a common language.

Dr. Albert Mehrabian of UCLA did the pioneering research in the field of body language. What he found was fascinating. He discovered that any given communication exchange contains three parts: the actual words you are speaking, the tone of voice you are using, and the less conscious body language that supports your message. Dr. Mehrabian found that what is actually *received* by the listener might surprise you. Of the entire message received, only 7% are the words, 38% is the tone of voice, and 55% is our body language! That means 93% of what is actually interpreted by those we communicate with has NOTHING to do with the words we are using! Scary, huh? We will soon learn how the subconscious mind is controlling far more than we have ever known, or probably want to believe.

Have you ever noticed during a conversation with someone that when you have your arms crossed within a few seconds the person crosses his or her arms as well? As the subconscious brain processes information, it is constantly trying to "connect" with the other person. As these studies show, it's really *how* a person is communicating that dictates the level of this subconscious connection. Sometimes, we can have the opposite effect by disconnecting with the other person.

My wife has a college friend who speaks in rapid-fire fashion. I can tell within seconds when she calls our house because my wife, who is normally a moderately paced, easy-to-follow speaker begins talking like she's reading a disclaimer at the end of a radio commercial. She isn't even aware she's doing it. It's her subconscious mirror neurons communicating to her friend that she is with her, accepts her, and is happy to be talking to her.

I have a friend—very intelligent, and a world traveler—whose speech pattern is maddening. He speaks like a machine gun, with very rapid bursts and draws odd and unusual examples out of thin air. Upon retrospect, his examples made sense, but I never had the time during a conversation to really apply what he said because I was always struggling to catch up! This example may hit a little too close to home for some salespeople.

On the other hand, I have another friend—likewise, very intelligent, someone who taught at college level—whose speech pattern is slower, but who zigzags from one digression to another, as if his brain were light years ahead of his mouth. By the time he ever gets to a point, you've forgotten what it was supposed to show! These examples lead us to the realization that there must be more to this "connection" thing than meets the eye.

"Effective communication is 20% what you know and 80% how you feel about what you know."
—JIM ROHN, author and motivational speaker

The Secrets of the "Buying" Brain

Retention of the information we communicate with customers is certainly important, but how does the brain actually process this information? The field of neuroscience has come leaps and bounds over the last decade to understand more clearly how we process information and make decisions. It's still a rapidly evolving science, but I believe we have enough new information today to equip you with the knowledge to become a more powerful connector.

We can describe the human brain as divided into three "layers." The outer layer is referred to as the neocortex. The middle area of the brain is the "limbic system" and the central core of the brain is what we call the "root brain." The neocortex and limbic layers are then subdivided into hemispheres conventionally called the "left and right brains." We will discuss the left and right brain of the two layers in more detail as the chapter unfolds.

To simplify the complex concepts of the neuroscience of the brain, we can regard the neocortex as the "thinking" brain. This is where all logic, rational thought, and fact processing occurs. The limbic brain can be characterized as the "feeling" brain. This is where emotion, feeling, visualization, and memories are housed.

Finally, the Root brain is known as the "instinctive" brain. This is where all instinctive responses and decisions are housed. When we communicate information, it is being processed through the appropriate senses and delivered initially to the root and limbic brain. It's there that we make an initial sub-conscious, emotion-based decision. We then use the neocortex to justify that decision with facts and logic. The relationship between the areas of the left and right brain has significant impact on this information processing as well.

Most people have been aware of this right-brain/left-brain phenomenon for decades, but it was not well understood. Just now researchers are finally penetrating the vast complexity of the human brain. It is of critical importance to understand the right-brain/left-brain separation and how it pertains to decision-making so that we can align our communication style with how our brain actually works. You've heard the phrase "A picture is worth a thousand words?" The right brain is the picture, and the left brain is the thousand words. Let's take a deeper look at the left brain/right brain concept.

Keep in mind that the field of neuroscience is advancing at the speed of light and we are uncovering new information nearly every month. To simplify things, it's important to know that the left and right brains talk to each other continually and collectively play a part in our conscious and subconscious thoughts and feelings.

However, through decades of studying split brain patients, we have arrived at the current conclusion that the left-brain activities include logic, factual organization, mathematics, defining, analyzing, diagnosing, articulating, problem solving, and documenting—to name a few.

Right-brain activities involve experimenting, visualizing, imagining, innovating, integrating, strategizing, observing, and risking emotion and feeling.

When it comes to interacting with other people, left-brain relating involves planning, organizing, managing, detailing, timing, implementing, supervising, controlling, and fixing. Right-brain relating involves teaching, communicating, counseling, supporting, understanding, persuading, and sensing others' needs.

Here is a classic example of the two approaches. The truck barrels through city streets until it comes to an overpass. But it is too tall by just an inch or so, and gets stuck. Quickly experts are summoned. Highway department officials hypothesize that perhaps there is a way to jack up the overpass with an elaborate network of jacks. (Have you guessed? These are the left-brain guys). Then a little boy comes along and says, "Gee mister, why don't you just let air out of the tires?" This is visualizing and observing, intuitively problem solving. Or . . . right brain! The left brain should take note: the right brain can sometimes save you money.

This is an inquisitive mind—a right-brain thought process applied to left-brain logic. The left-brain automatically breaks down all holistic entities into elements along the lines of 3D logic, and this, in turn, causes a 3D consciousness. We see what happens in medicine when doctors, who are extremely logical sorts, get wedded to a 3D consciousness. They focus solely on healing the disease as defined by the external symptoms or tests, but often neglect natural healing paths that would come from right-brain intuitive thought.

That's why everyone liked the cranky "Dr. House" on television so much. Even though he seemed the epitome of left-brain rational thinking, it was his "hunches" that he knew evidence would eventually support—but which at the time he acted did not usually have any proof—that produced the cure.

College textbooks are usually arranged along the lines of a left-brain approach, either sequentially or chronologically. Yet we are confronted almost daily with "illogical" realities: if you go into a skid on the ice, turn *into* the skid. Tax *cuts* cause the wealthy to pay higher total taxes. A Chinese finger trap requires you to push *inward* to escape, rather than pulling away.

This of course does not mean that there are not facts and truth. Nor does it mean "two plus two equals five" just because you want it to! Much of our education system today has gone completely in the other direction by emphasizing "self-esteem," without appreciating that self-esteem comes from achievement and overcoming obstacles, not by false praise for answers even the student knows is wrong. The goal is to involve the right brain without abandoning the necessary elements of the left-brain.

There are two photographs of Albert Einstein that capture this perfectly. In one that represents the left brain, Einstein, the intellectual, stares ahead soberly, as if contemplating the origin of the universe. But another—the right-brain photo—shows a silly Einstein, hair askew, eyes laughingly open, sticking his tongue out.

Which is the real Albert Einstein? The answer is both: we all have both sides of the brain upon which to draw, but often fall into the habit of using only our left brain. Remember our communication evolution in the previous chapter? That's right, it's been trained into us.

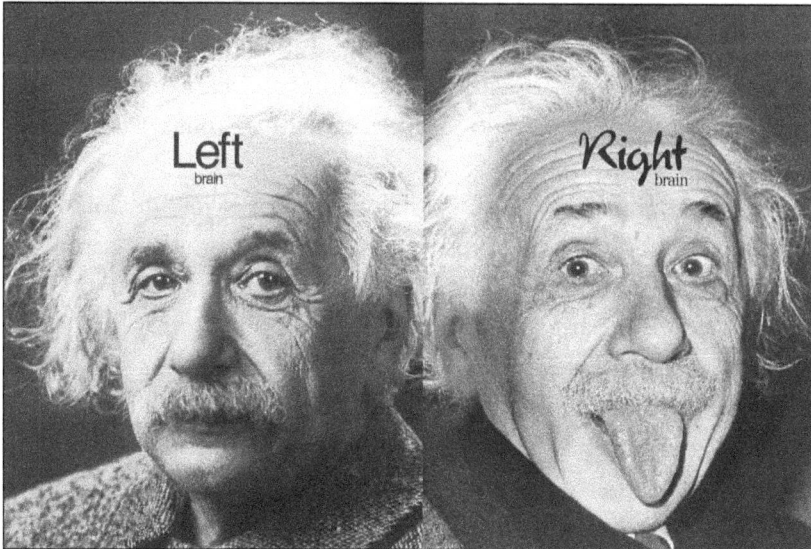

Knowing how the brain processes information helps us to understand why leveraging stories and visual forms of communication drives the greatest impact and connection with the customer.

John P. Kotter, a best-selling author of leadership books and professor at Harvard Business School, said "Over the years I have become convinced that we learn best—and change—from hearing stories that strike a chord within us.... Those in leadership positions who fail to grasp or use the power of stories risk failure for their companies and for themselves."[10] Blake Mycoski, the CEO of Tom's Shoes, agreed: "I realized the importance of having a story today is what really separates companies. People don't just wear our shoes, they tell our story."[11]

Red Brain, Blue Brain . . . Pink Brain, New Brain

Daniel Pink argued in his book, *A Whole New Mind*, that "Right-Brained People Will Rule the Future,"[12] and that we are moving from an information age (where the logical, sequential, and analytic left brain dominates) to a conceptual age powered by the inventive, empathetic, and big picture skills of the right side of the brain. He goes on to say, "We are our stories. We compress years of experience, view, and emotion into a few compact narratives that we convey to others and tell to ourselves."

Pink is supported by Alan Brinkley, former Provost at Columbia University, who wrote that while science and technology aspire to crisp, clear answers, the humanities address ambiguity, doubt, and skepticism.[13] Both are essential in today's world. Logic, notes Noel Huntley, is only three-dimensional, and he claims that a society that is "left-brain" centered eventually ends up in conflict and disharmony. The right brain is suppressed by left-brain thinkers, yet it is the source for all discovery and innovation.

According to several neuro-researchers, the human brain can perform close to twenty petaflop (twenty quadrillion) calculations per second.[14] I don't know about you, but I have no concept—left- or right-brained—as to just how large that number is!

If that's true, and it appears that it is, how many of those calculations can you *consciously* focus on at one time? If you're like me, the answer is ONE! That means there are twenty quadrillion calculations (minus one) happening at the subconscious level. It's as if there's an army of people buried deep inside our brains operating completely independent of our command and control. Scary, isn't it?

For those who are familiar with Daniel Kahneman's book *Thinking Fast and Slow*, you know he discusses the conscious and subconscious brain in the form of two systems. System two represents the conscious mind and what we would call more neocortex processing. System one is referred to as more of the subconscious mind or in our language, more closely aligned to the limbic and root brain areas. Regardless of how you slice and dice the brain, it comes down to "Thinking," "Feeling," and "Instinctive," "Conscious and Subconscious," and "Left and Right."

Now that we are armed with this significant information, what does it mean to our communication style? It means we need to take our newly dissected brains and begin to prioritize which parts have the largest impact on connection and decision-making.

Decision-making pathways are extremely complicated, and there is still some debate among the neuroscience community as to where exactly this process is housed within the brain. What we do understand, however, is that at a very primitive level, all decisions come down to one of two emotional categories. Self-preservation or pleasure. In other words, will the decision I'm about to make cause me potential "pain" or provide me with some form of "gain"?

I will discuss further the limbic brain, but the basic theory is that decisions actually take place in the instinctive "root brain" with heavy influences from the emotional-centered right limbic brain, much to the chagrin of our logical, rational, left brain of the neocortex with its well thought-out and carefully researched perceptions. The left brain, specifically in the neocortex, does the job of analyzing the facts, but it's the right brain (in the root and limbic) that ends up calling the shots, on an instinctive and emotional level. The left-brain neocortex then kicks back in gear to help execute the decision and supports the emotional decision with facts and logic.

Have you ever said the phrase, "I just don't have a good gut *thought* about that guy . . ." Of course not. You say, "I just don't have a good gut *feeling* about that guy."

Once we understand that emotion and trust are built primarily in the root and limbic right brain, we can target our communication to illicit those types of responses. Decisions aren't based on what we *think*; they're a response to how we *feel*. Do you know where the optic nerve terminates in the brain? If you guessed the "root brain," you win the prize.

Now that we know that visual imagery is triggered and processed in the root brain as well, then it stands to reason that in order to create trust and connection, we must use a visual communication style. Facts and statistics are cold and lifeless and are interpreted by the left-brain neocortex. Visual images travel the optic nerve straight to the root brain where the information is processed at lightning speed by our instinctive brain, colored with a bit of feeling and emotion from our limbic brain and decisions are made immediately.

Now you know why you are able to run within milliseconds of seeing a snake before your logical neocortex can "think" to rationalize your decision. We used to think that only fight or flight decisions were made this way. It turns out all decisions happen this way in varying degrees based on the time afforded to process the "facts" later.

When it comes to communication, the facts certainly matter; however, when we wrap our factual information around stories, analogies, metaphors, and visual aids, we drive the listener to the root brain and right side of the limbic brain. It is here, even subconsciously, that they connect with us. The listener is actually completely unaware that this phenomenon is taking place. They begin to trust you . . . even start to like you . . . yet they can't put their finger on exactly why.

Conversely, when you communicate with facts, figures, and statistics, the listener's process-oriented left brain and neocortex instinctively becomes skeptical of those facts. It's just how we are wired. And if the listener is subconsciously skeptical of your facts and data guess what else they are subconsciously skeptical of? YOU!

To sum up this hemispheric conundrum: we have been trained to count, list, sequentially develop, and logically examine and explain everything. This has deprived us of the emotional, intuitive, right-brained, non-linear elements of our education and our communication. These are the most crucial elements of all.

To bring it back to sales or business, consider your typical presentation with statistics and logical reasoning. Have you caused your audience to *care or feel* a certain way about your information or your product? What have you done in your talk, or your sales pitch, or your briefing, to motivate and excite the target of your efforts? It is here where most communication efforts fail, and often fail miserably.

Information presented without proper visual motivation does not have direction. Peg Neuhauser, a business consultant, once noted, "No tribal chief or elder has ever handed out statistical reports, charts, graphs, or lists of facts to explain where a group is headed or what it must do." She could have added, "or PowerPoint presentations." A communication that fails to visually stimulate and motivate will almost certainly ensure that your report sits on a desk, or that your order form is never filled out.

We routinely fall back on statistics and charts. You may say, "I thought the facts and statistics *were* the motivation. Doesn't the possibility of increased sales or market share spur people to act?" Occasionally, yes. More often than not, though, you cement the statistics *through* the story.

Cognitive psychologist Jerome Bruner once said, "A fact is twenty times more likely to be remembered if it is anchored in narrative."[15] Knowledge—facts—are the easiest things for people to change, which is why we are generally skeptical of them. A visual image, on the other hand, that we've created in our own mind around those facts *has* to be believable because *WE* are the ones that created the image! If you can't trust yourself, whom can you trust?

If I asked you what color my Papaw's truck was in my original introduction story, would you remember? How old was I in the story? What did he die from? These are all facts. In our workshop, I ask these questions toward the end of the first day. Everyone always gets the answers right. Why? Because the facts were intentionally woven *into* the story. We suspect today that the human brain has a finite capacity for facts and statistics but an infinite capacity for visual imagery.

You may have forgotten a couple of the details of my Papaw's story depending on how long ago you read that portion of the book, but I can assure you, when hearing the story live, with emotion, tone, and body language all playing their proper role, the listener never forgets details.

"A fact is twenty times more likely to be remembered if it is anchored in narrative."
—JEROME BRUNER, clinical psychologist

Sometimes, our brains can be *too* good at filling in the visual blanks. Have you ever had a situation where you had a memory of many years ago that you had been to some event like a movie or family get-together? You were *sure* that you saw a certain movie with another person, or that Uncle Harry was at the party. Yet when you talk with others who were at the event, it becomes clear you were mistaken.

Do you continue to hold the erroneous view of the past? No. You replace your wrong data set—your memory, in this case—with the new (correct) facts around the story. You'll probably even laugh about it later. "Yeah, you know, I could have sworn Harry was at that party. Harry was at sea on a cruise then! Shows how wrong I was." If you don't communicate with a story-based approach, your customers will fill in the details of your engagement to suit *their* narrative and there's a chance it won't be the story you were hoping for.

When it comes to the brain producing images, you can either paint the picture for the customer, or they will paint it themselves. If you continue to use facts and statistics to "paint your picture" you will continue to get blank stares. Your customers are wired just like you. They are instinctively visual, and if you aren't communicating to them in a visual language, they are much more prone to let their minds wander off into a picture that's already in their heads. And you can be assured that the picture has nothing to do with you or your products!

Most good sales people and CEOs do not need a disaster before they accept new knowledge. On the contrary, it becomes part and parcel of their work—evaluating reports, statistics, data, and above all listening to the advice of others. *What* they hear will be up to you. That is your area of expertise. But *how* they hear it is where I can help you. Since we know the average person communicates transactionally with facts and figures, how much will you be able to differentiate yourself from the average person by using a different approach? Significantly.

So how do you influence people to a specific course of action for mutual benefit? Rational or logical arguments rarely work if someone has been behaviorally committed to a process. Consider smokers. How many of them really do not know that it harms their health? But does that stop them? The mind can always rationalize that "I'm one of the 100 out of 1,000 who will not get lung cancer." Yet our usual first line of attack when it comes to changing someone's mind is logic or reason. We'll explore this more in the objection-handling chapter. For those who would like a little more detail, let's go deeper into the areas of the brain we've been discussing.

The Limbic "Filter"

How do we internally compress our years of emotion and experience into these narratives that we tell ourselves and tell others? What does that look like? You've heard "we are the sum of our experiences." What does that really mean? Let's dig even deeper into the science behind that, and look at where our emotional "cells" are located—in what we call the limbic "filter," but, as you might have guessed, I'd like to introduce this with a story.

A few years ago I was taking my daughter on a field trip. I climbed on a school bus, and thought about how I have always had the "heebie-jeebies" about getting on school buses. Why was that?

Then I remembered that from kindergarten to fourth grade, we had a bully on our school bus. He would do things like push people down and knock the books out of your hand, the typical bullying behavior. I processed those experiences through my limbic system, specifically my hippocampus and amygdala, and internalized that experience into my cognitive long-term memory over the years. It was still with me as an adult.

Once I realized what was causing my reaction, I could overcome it. All of us have these persuasive sub-conscious memories. They are what I have affectionately termed "junk in the brain trunk." And our trunk is the limbic filter, and every person in the world has one.

It's through this "filter" that the brain creates an association of physical sensations to produce memories of an emotional state. It guides our reason and logic toward outcomes that make us happy and perhaps in earlier times ensured our self-preservation. This is the area of the brain where I earlier referenced our most primitive decision-making process.

As I have mentioned, every decision you've ever made or will ever make essentially comes down to preventing pain or achieving gain. These are both "feelings" or "emotions" that are housed in the right side of the limbic brain. When our senses enter information, usually it is of a non-consensual variety—you remember the pain of touching a hot stove, the pleasure of your first real kiss, the excitement of a roller coaster, the horror of going in the "deep end" before you were ready and thinking you'd drown.

We almost all had that irritating aunt who used to come up and pinch our cheek, or the gregarious uncle who thought he was being funny when he gave you a "Dutch rub." These experiences are all sorted and stored by the limbic system, which influences the endocrine system and autonomic nervous system to produce highs, lows, fear, desire, and so on.

Some of these functions can save your life ("flight or fight" reflex). Others help you choose a mate ("all I remember was he took my breath away"). Still others provide you with those "hunches" you have about certain situations ("I just didn't have a good feeling about doing business with that guy").

Ahhh . . . remember how we discussed earlier the difference between a "gut thought" versus a "gut *feeling*?" Now you know where that sensation arises and takes hold. Another important point to note is that speech is housed in the left brain, and the limbic area has no capacity for speech. This is why we can easily become "speechless" when we see something that moves us emotionally. When they told me my Papaw had passed away, I was emotionally moved to the point of speechlessness. This is why feelings are so much harder to express than thoughts. I will refrain from citing the countless cheesy love song lyrics that illustrate this point.

When it comes to people, the limbic "filter" kicks into action immediately with your first impression. Have you ever heard "you never get a second chance to make a first impression?" While that's true in the narrowest sense of the phrase, of course people can "grow on you," and of course you can change your opinion about people. (How often have you heard a happy couple say "We couldn't stand each other when we first met"?)

Still, it is difficult to overcome bad first impressions. How long do you have to make this pivotal first impression? Some research shows you have *one-tenth of a second!* Other researchers give up to thirty seconds for someone to form a first impression of you.[16] Either way, before you even really meet someone, it is already determined how that person will respond to you by your dress, your attitude, your gestures, and your walk. If you don't have it going *on* when you're going *in*, it's likely too late. When we speak of

> "It's the strangest part of being famous because you don't get to give first impressions anymore. Everyone already has an impression of you before you meet them."
> —KRISTEN STEWART
> *Entertainment Weekly* interview, November 2011

"prejudice," it's impossible to avoid—by nature. Everyone "discriminates" instantaneously, without even consciously realizing it, due to *experiences* he or she has had in the past (the junk in our brain trunk).

Many times you are not even aware of those experiences (hence, the booming business for "shrinks" in America, whose primary tool is to get you to unlock those past experiences so you can understand where the "feeling" is coming from and gain power over it). It's this "awareness" of the junk in the brain trunk that allowed me to bypass its negative subconscious control over my school bus heebie-jeebies—and what is really behind all of our emotional responses.

Your first impression of someone begins with a mental image, a form of social processing, and research shows it can be quite accurate.[17] Psychologists call the brain circuitry that bypasses the neocortex the "amygdala hijack"—in other words, your intuition kicks in before your logic can assess all the data. This of course stemmed from the need in more primitive or frontier societies to determine quickly if someone posed a threat. Perhaps more distressing, this process works whether you interact with someone in person or on video.

An article in the May 29, 2000 issue of *The New Yorker* magazine reports on how social psychologists have demonstrated that it takes only about ten to fifteen seconds of videotape for someone to form a lasting impression about another person. In this case, students ranked the performance of various teachers. Their snap impressions consistently matched up with those of other students who evaluated the same professors after spending an entire semester in their classrooms. This tells you how powerful the limbic filter is and how it drives subconscious decision-making.

So far, we've discussed retention capacity, the three layers of the brain (neocortex, limbic, and root), the left-brain/right-brain phenomena, body language, and first impressions. Nearly every piece of this communication is happening as part of the twenty quadrillion minus one calculations being performed by the *subconscious* mind. What does all this process usually lead to? Anxiety.

This is Your Brain on Neuro-Chemicals

According to anxietycentre.com, 40 million people in the United States will experience impairment because of an anxiety condition this year. Two of the top-10 best-selling prescription drugs on the market today are used to treat anxiety, and anti-depression prescriptions have risen 400 percent since 1988. I have friends and family who are on these medications, and odds are many of you reading this book are as well.

What actually drives anxiety? *Webster*'s dictionary defines anxiety as: *"an abnormal and overwhelming sense of apprehension and fear often marked by physiological signs (as sweating, tension, and increased pulse), driven by doubt concerning the reality and nature of the threat, and by self-doubt about one's capacity to cope with it."* As my friend and leadership expert Ford Taylor describes it, anxiety is a fear of failure fighting against your own desire and motivation to succeed. Anxiety can be crippling. Left unchecked, it can actually lead to severe health issues.

Anxiety leads to our next communication crippler—stress. Did you know that the emotional and physical responses you have to stress are set in motion by a series of chemical releases and reactions? The following explanation is taken from the Franklin Institute's Resource for Science Learning:

Attack of the Adrenals: A Metabolic Story

The ambulance siren screams its warning to get out of the way. You can't move your car because you're stuck in a bumper-to-bumper traffic jam that reaches as far as the eye can see. There must be an accident up ahead. Meanwhile the road construction crew a few feet from your car is jack-hammering the pavement. You are about to enter the stress zone. Inside your body the alert goes out: "Attention all parasympathetic forces. Urgent. Adrenal gland missile silos mounted atop kidneys have just released chemical *cortisol* weapons of brain destruction. Mobilize all internal defenses.

Launch immediate counter-calm hormones before hippocampus is hammered by cortisol."

Hormones rush to your adrenal glands to suppress the streaming cortisol on its way to your brain. Other hormones rush to your brain to round up all the remnants of cortisol missiles that made it to your hippocampus. These hormones escort the cortisol remnants back to Kidneyland for a one-way ride on the Bladderhorn. You have now reached metabolic equilibrium, also known as homeostasis.[18]

The Anxiety Highway

The above illustration may or may not resonate with you, but this cascade of events is happening to everyone to one extent or another multiple times a day. Your sympathetic nervous system, triggered in the limbic system "filter" kicks in at a moment's notice and alerts your adrenal glands to release adrenaline and other hormones that increase breathing, heart rate, and blood pressure. This is part of the familiar "fight or flight" mechanism we have all heard about.

As the newly increased oxygen-rich blood is carried faster to the brain, your body is physically prepared to take some form of aggressive action. This "metabolic overdrive" state that your body is in causes stress, releases other compounds like cortisol into the system and essentially disables the brain from functioning in a normal, relatively calm state.

So what's the effect on our communication during this time? For communicators, one of the two types of stress: distress or eustress, kicks in. The word "stress" is actually short for distress, which is Latin for "to draw or pull apart." So when we're under *distress*, it can feel like we're literally being pulled apart mentally and, at times, physically. This plays out in our communication in a variety of ways from causing one to stutter or stammer over words to literally falling quiet. It also causes our brain to become completely inward focused and self-absorbed. This is why so many salespeople struggle with objections. Your subconscious mind is chemically fighting your conscious mind for control through this anxiety and stress cascade.

Now, when *eustress* kicks in, this is known as "good" stress. "Eu" is Greek for . . . you guessed it . . . good. First coined by endocrinologist Hans Selye, this good stress happens to us when we get overly excited and generally mani-fests itself in the form of feeling purpose, hope, or vigor. Too much of this "good" stress can also be an impediment to our communication. How, you might ask? Well, you can have too much of a good thing. When a salesperson is experiencing eus-tress, he or she tends to ramble incessantly and barely pause to breathe. This type of stress literally "amps" you up. You tend to feel energized and excitable.

> "A crust eaten in peace is better than a banquet partaken in anxiety."
> —AESOP
> *The Town Mouse and the Country Mouse*

When I used to coach my daughter's basketball team, I could always tell which girls were suffering from distress versus the girls under the control of eustress. The distressed girls generally shot air balls due to the inhibitory effects of the stress. My eustress girls on the other hand, would shoot the ball over the basket at times, overrun plays, and generally be a spastic mess. Once I saw how each girl reacted, I could coach them appropriately based on their specific stress. When we begin to identify this stress in ourselves, we can begin to gain back control from our subconscious army and begin to "coach" ourselves back to a state of normalcy.

Can cortisol be an ally in our story-based approach? Believe it or not, yes. If just the right amount of cortisol is released in the brain, it can actually cause the listener to focus more closely on the story at hand.

Dr. Paul Zak found recently in his research that two primary chemicals are released during an effective story: cortisol and oxyto-cin.[19] When a story has the right amount of conflict or tension, corti-sol is released by the brain of the listener causing them to focus and pay attention to your narrative. Interestingly, when the listener has really connected with the speaker, oxytocin gets released. We have learned now that oxytocin is the primary chemical associated with empathy and trust. If a customer has empathy for you and a trust in you, then you have certainly accomplished your goal of connecting! Do you think facts and figures cause one to release oxytocin? Quite the opposite. What triggers this release most effectively? You might have guessed . . . stories!

Whew . . . let's take a left-brained breath. That's probably more neuroscience than many of you have had in a lifetime! Yes, I recognize the irony that I'm proposing an entire shift to having more, right-brain-centric communication from the root brain, and then explained it with an entire chapter laden with science about the neocortex and left brain! Hopefully, you related to enough of the illustrations, analogies, and metaphors to keep your right brain engaged. It's important that you have this scientific foundation in order for you to truly "buy in" to the methodology.

I think you can now see that there is way more than meets the eye when it comes to communication. From the moment we step out of our vehicle to walk into a prospective customer's office, our subconscious mind is striving for control. From anxiety to stress to first impressions to body language, so much happens before we even open our mouths! After this, we engage with our customers in one direction or another. Are we going to be factual, logical, and left-brained as usual, or with a new and improved visual, emotional, right-brained approach? All the while, our limbic filter is processing, processing, processing.

Guess what else is happening that we haven't even acknowledged to this point? Your customer is experiencing the exact same things. Anxiety, stress, limbic-filter processing, and first impressions—it's overwhelming to think about, isn't it? In the next chapter we will dive into how all this neuroscience stuff impacts the actual decision-making process. Now we are getting somewhere.

WHAT'S *YOUR* STORY?

❋ *Think of your last three sales interactions. Did you communicate using left-brain facts and data? Be honest . . .*

❋ *Imagine the last major purchase you made. Describe your thought process in the decision. Now describe how it made you feel. Notice any difference?*

❋ *How many training sessions have you attended that taught you how to memorize facts and information?*

❋ *Can you take all the facts and information you've memorized and tell a story with them?*

❋ *What "junk in your brain trunk" do you have that has the strongest influence on how you view and interact with the world around you?*

3

The SBS (Story-Based Selling) Tackle Box

"You're Gonna Need a Bigger Boat"

—Captain Brody, *Jaws*

We all have stories. Our right brains are constantly processing mini-movies all day, every day. Some of us are more "natural" storytellers, and for others it takes a bit more effort. Either way, in order to be a master at SBS, you will need to expand your repertoire and become more intentional with your story-based communication. Every great writer has a "process" by which they craft their masterpieces. Every great filmmaker has a "system" by which he attempts to visually communicate and translate the words of a screenplay onto the big screen.

To be a great story-based communicator, you need tools as well. This chapter is designed to expand your "tackle box" in order to land bigger "fish" and do it more often. This is where the left brain and the right brain come together to create your very own personalized "process." Your left brain will maintain order while your right brain is released to create, imagine, and connect. This chapter will introduce you to the "Categories," "Elements," and "Techniques" you will use to create your SBS Story Life Lines.

"Imagination is more important than knowledge."
—Albert Einstein
Cosmic Religion: With Other Opinions and Aphorisms

We have seen that when you meet someone—such as a customer or client—you have seconds to make a first impression on that person. And we have seen how the brain processes these impressions, so we next have to establish how you can best *make* that first impression. It involves a whole lot more than the old John Malloy book, *Dress for Success*!

The first thing to remember is that facts and figures, reasoning, and logic do not make the connection. A story does. You have a story to tell—you have *your* story to tell. But there is a challenge: your customer *also* has a story, and your competitors will have a story of their own. You must take those into consideration.

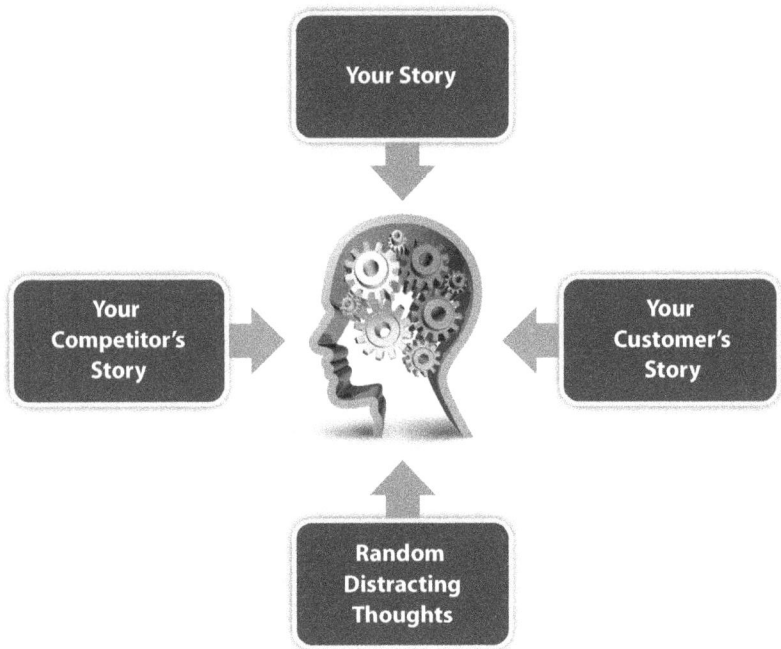

Competing for the Mind of Your Customer

On top of that, you will always have distractions, such as a waiter interrupting at a key moment, an assistant coming into an office with an urgent message, or even (unfortunately) cell phones and text messages that people seem forced to look at. Perhaps you aren't a comic, but almost everyone remembers a time while telling a joke, when just at the moment you're about to deliver the punch line, someone interrupts. Your listener, distracted, soon turns back to you and says, "I'm sorry. Now, where were we?" *That joke is dead.* That story can never be recovered, or at least not anytime soon. So how do you get your story across those barriers?

The Synchronization of Two Brains Communicatin'

Let's look at the process of communication. This is what I call the Thoughts-Emotions-Decision Cascade. Realize that all communication will produce thoughts that triggers some form of emotion or feeling, and this will happen in *seconds*. When you communicate information to a listener, it forms an impression (in seconds). The listener then subconsciously transforms that information into a thought, which he or she then automatically turns into an emotion. It is this emotion—not the information—that triggers a decision.

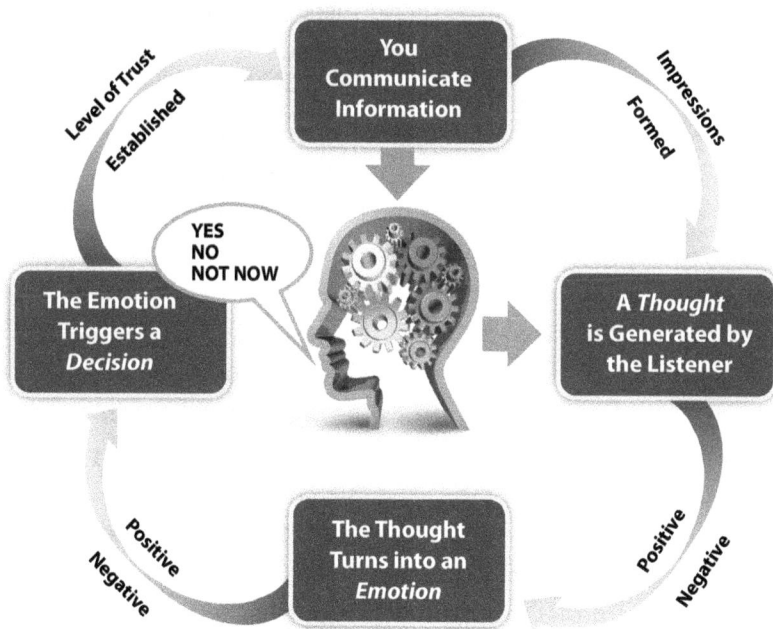

Thoughts-Emotions-Decisions Cascade

We know that the average communicator walks into a meeting and immediately begins with facts. "Hello Mr. Jones, I'm Sandra Smith, and I'd like to explain to you how my company can help your company save money. First . . ." You already know where this approach comes from, right? The left brain. It is transactional communication. What is transmitted is a left-brain thought that instantly turns into an emotion of uncertainty, skepticism, or ambivalence ("hmm. I'm being 'sold' here!"), and this emotion triggers a decision ("no, not now," etc.).

Not only do you not achieve your immediate goal, but the interaction has now also produced a lack of trust. Remember, this is not intentional on the part of the listener. It's happening at the subconscious level as the brain runs those twenty quadrillion calculations.

From that first engagement and moving forward, whenever Mr. Jones sees Sandra Smith his emotions tell him "she's out to sell me something." Even if the person actually buys the product or hires the service, there will be underlying insecurity that typically leads to buyer's remorse, and the relationship is dead.

But what happens if you begin with a story? We'll deal with questions and objections later, but I know you will immediately have this response: "What if I tell the wrong story? What if I tell the story of my favorite puppy who died and I learned how important it is to care for animals and the weak—and this person just lost a pet?" *Even if you tell the wrong story—one that perhaps elicits an immediate emotional reaction that isn't good for you—you have still elicited trust by showing your vulnerability.* The process has still been moved from the left brain to the right brain. You may have missed a field goal, but you have changed stadiums, and you now have home-field advantage.

I have heard countless stories from people who have been through the Story-Based Selling live workshop about their leaving a sales call feeling like they totally blew it by telling a story that bombed, only to get a call from the customer inviting them back for a second appointment or, better yet, chose them for the deal.

In fact, I recently heard from a former SBS participant's manager that after his rep supposedly "bombed" with his attempt to tell a story, the manager overheard a phone call from the customer who actually said the reason they called the rep back was because they felt a connection and trusted him ... even though their product was technologically inferior to the competitor's! The manager went on to say, "This Story-Based Selling stuff really works.

A story-based sales professional communicates through visuals to express good values, experiences, and clarity of purpose. This in turn generates the listener's thoughts of security, enlightenment, and a good "gut feeling," which turns into a positive emotion. And this triggers your goal of a "yes" decision—based on a calm comprehension of the situation and an enhanced level of trust."

Once you have moved your listener onto your home field, you'll find your story is not only heard, but elicits the response and connection you want. In sales there is always talk about "closing," but it really is as simple as this.

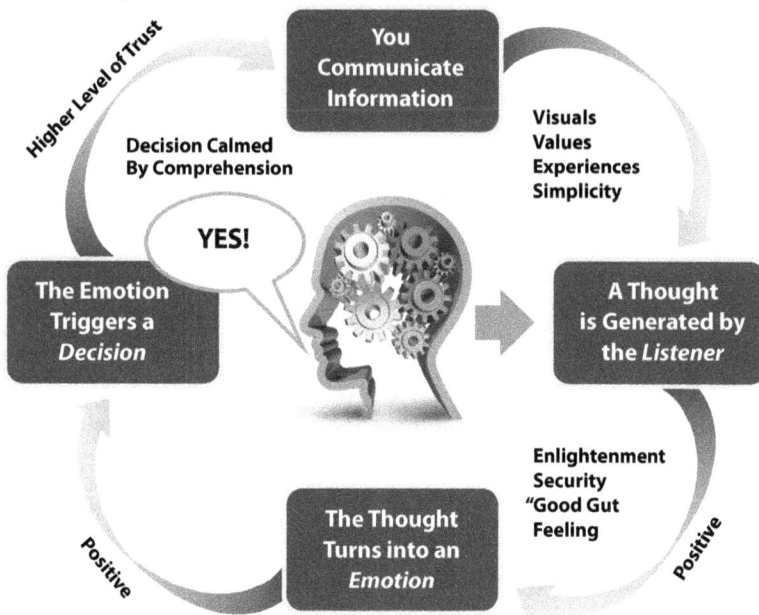

Story-Based Selling Communication Approach

The irony to this approach, however, is that ultimately we have to provide you with a process—which is left-brained! Remember Daniel-san and Mr. Miagi in "Karate Kid?" Mr. Miagi had Daniel sand the floor, paint the fence, wax the car—all of which were processes that seemingly had nothing whatsoever to do with learning karate. But when the moment arrived, he had been provided with tools that were perfectly appropriate for Daniel to drop the "crane" on Johnny and win the match!

So we have to provide you the tools for you to tell effective stories. And, as you might guess, we're going to begin by telling two stories (two tools in your tool-box), one a "relation-focused" story and the other a "persuasion-focused" story. You might not "get" where we're going here, but that's ok. After I explain the elements and techniques to you, we will come back and analyze each.

RELATION-FOCUSED stories are those that build relationships, gain trust, and demonstrate personal or company vulnerability.

As you read the following story, focus on how it makes you *feel*, rather than what you might be *thinking*.

> When we were first married, my wife and I were excited about having a family. We weren't entirely sure how soon that would happen, but after just a year of marriage we became pregnant with our first child, a baby girl. I wasn't sure how to be a dad, and quite honestly, I was terrified. How would I take care of her, provide for her, and protect her in a world that seemed to be spinning recklessly out of control like a car hitting a frozen patch of road doing 100 mph? I was overwhelmed by the magnitude of the responsibility, but entirely consumed by the love I had for this new incredible human being.

I will never forget when the nurse wrapped her in the blanket and laid her in my trembling arms that first day. She looked up at me with those big, bright eyes and seemed to say without speaking, "I love you, daddy, and I can't wait for you to start teaching me about life."

Three months later, I was hit with a harsh and sobering reality. The doctor walked into the cold, small exam room with stark, white walls, put the CT scans up on the back-lit board and confirmed what I had dreaded to hear but had suspected. I had cancer. I sat in my car in the hospital parking lot as the sleet/rain mix pelted my windshield and bawled like a baby. Images of my wife and newborn daughter raced through my head. How could this be happening? Who would take care of them?

The irony of the situation, as you may remember from previous stories in this book, was that I worked in bio-tech and knew oncology extremely well. I knew the stories and I knew the clinical outcomes. I knew the best doctors and I knew the best protocols. Quite honestly, it calmed me beyond comprehension.

I was diagnosed at a very early stage and believed I could be cured. It didn't stop me from worrying, and it didn't stop me from having a breakdown or two along the way, but it helped me to stay focused. I was determined to be there to teach my daughter how to shoot a basketball and have her teach me how to dance like a ballerina. I was resolute in my picture of walking her down the aisle and eventually spoiling the daughter she would one day have. I wanted to be a part of *her* story.

As you might have guessed by the fact that I'm still around to write this book, I made it. I was cured. I *have* taught my beautiful and talented daughter, Gracie, how to shoot a basketball and she has become one of the most graceful dancers I have ever seen (though teaching me how to dance like a ballerina was a task no human could achieve.)

And just to keep the story exciting, we've added a little brother to the mix to keep her on her toes. Life has a funny way of throwing you curve balls, but it also has a way of teaching you perspective and priorities. It may be a cliché, but every day is a gift to me, and I love nothing more than to be a character in my kids' stories . . . for as long as the good Lord allows, or until they get tired of me, whichever one comes first!

Now, with that story fresh in our minds, let's shift gears to our second category of story, the persuasion-focused story.

PERSUASION-FOCUSED stories are designed to elicit a specific course of action by connecting visual solutions to subconscious needs.

The following story is a real-world example taken from an interaction between a sales representative and a physician:

Dr. Smith, let me tell you about Martha. She was fifty-four years-old when she found out she was going to be a grandmother for the first time. She was ecstatic. Her oldest daughter, Emily, had recently moved back to town with her husband, Eric. Martha couldn't have been more excited. She not only had her baby back in town, but now her grandbaby would be a mere five minutes away!

The weekend following the big move, Martha began to notice a problem. She and Emily were riding bikes on the neighborhood bike path and she couldn't seem to catch her breath. She didn't think too much of it but as the week wore on she felt extremely lethargic and began to have a persistent cough. She just assumed she had picked up a virus. It made her think about how important it was to stay healthy because the baby would be here in a mere six months and she would want to spend as much time as possible with that beautiful child.

One week ran into two, which ran into three, and she couldn't shake her lethargy or cough. She finally broke down and went to see her primary care physician. He sent her for a few tests and a CT scan of her chest.

When the doctor called her the next day, she dropped the phone and crumbled to a heap on the floor. It was stage-four small cell lung cancer. Her prognosis was grim. She was given just three to six months to live. But the baby was coming in five months. Her thoughts raced to what options she had. She made up her mind that day that she would fight it and fight it as hard as she could. She was determined to be there when they brought that baby home.

(Let's see how we would transition this story for persuasion purposes.)

Doctor Smith: I'm not sure how many fifty-four-year-old, soon-to-be grandmas you have in your practice with this diagnosis, but our drug "cure-all" has proven in randomized, placebo-controlled clinical trials to extend the life of patients just like Martha by up to eighteen months. How valuable do you think these extra months would be for your patients like Martha?

As you can see, the purpose of this story isn't just about creating relationship, it's about driving the "buyer" to the right side of the brain and giving them an emotional connection from which to make a decision. Once you do this, you begin to *earn the right* to present the "facts" and become a little more transactional.

In the case of the Martha story, after the last question, you could easily explain all the clinical endpoints of the "cure-all" trial and

Dr. Smith would receive those "statistics" in a much different light. You can insert any product or service and see how this type of story really moves the listener into the receptive right brain and allows the person to visualize the impact of the solution you will eventually suggest. Remember, as Jerome Bruner stated, "A fact is twenty times more likely to be remembered when wrapped in a narrative."

Generally, I recommend beginning engagements with relation-focused stories before transitioning to persuasion-focused stories. No matter how good you become at persuasion-focused stories, you will still eventually ask for a decision. The more trust that's been built through relation-focused stories, the easier that decision will come.

Now that you know the difference, let's explore further exactly how you build a story. I know by now my left-brained, transactional readers are craving a list, so I will deviate from the right brain just long enough to introduce you to the **Five Elements** of Story-Based Selling:

- Have a **Purpose** with passion. What is the objective of telling the story? Do you mean it, or are you reciting something?

- Make a **Connection**—people connect, and it's critical that your story have a point of connection. It may be hard to connect with someone who has never played golf by telling a golf story, so go with what will work for most people, such as personal experiences that others likely have gone through. Remember, never tell a story without a point and try your best to never make a point without a connecting story.

- Usually, there is a **Barrier or Conflict**—somewhere, you must identify an obstacle that the listener feels and sees the need to overcome, and it must have relevance to your listener.

- Then you will arrive at the **Aha Factor**. This is a moment of awareness where the listener sees a solution to the problem or conflict you identified above. It is important that the listener feels he has come to this "Aha" moment by himself, not that you have imposed it on him.

- That leads you to a **Resolution**, where the listener is drawn to a conclusion or course of action.

The key to a great story is to have these elements flow into what we call the "Story Lifeline."

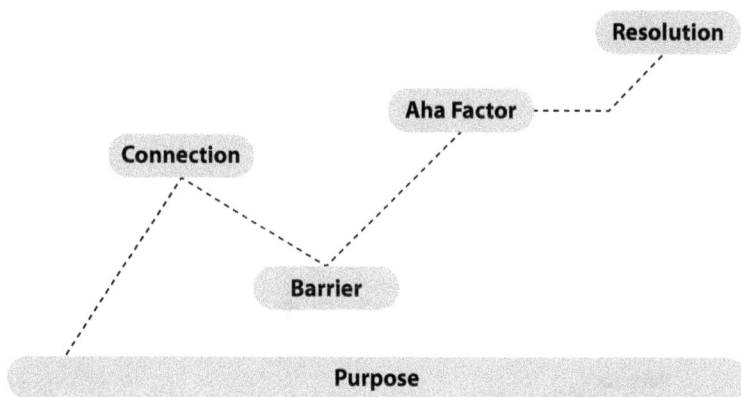

Story-Based Selling Story Lifeline

The Story Lifeline is the "road map" that keeps you on track and keeps your listener engaged. Many of us learned about the story "arc" concept in English class years ago. The Story Lifeline is similar in concept but differs greatly in overall intention. During communication, particularly in sales, the goal is to have a purpose for each story, create a connection, introduce the barrier or conflict, reveal the Aha factor and bring the story to resolution, which creates an action in the mind of the customer. The key difference from there is that the next interaction, whether in the same call or subsequent calls, should build upon the previous one.

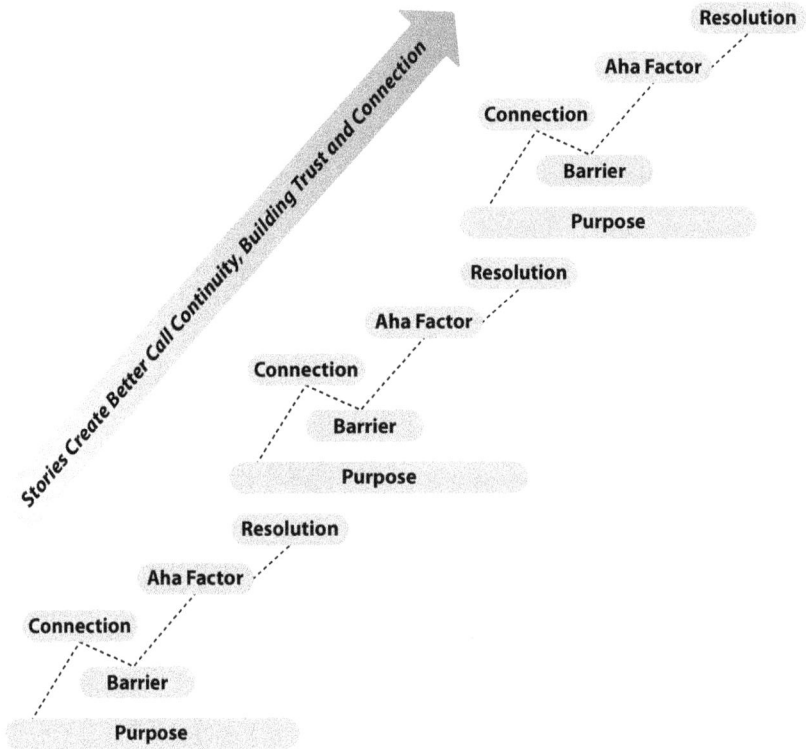

SBS Trust Building Continuum

To achieve these five elements of the Story Lifeline road map, you can use any of **Four Techniques** to tell your story.

Technique of Using a Personal Illustration

First, and most obvious, is the technique of giving a **personal illustration**. Relate a situation from your own life where you overcame a barrier, arrived at an "aha" moment, and resolved it. Just for fun, let's go back to grammar school. Remember point of view? There are three basic perspectives from which a story is told: First person, second person, and third person. In first person, the voice of the story is immersed in the action. *I saved the world today with my quick thinking.* Second person is told directly to the reader. *You saved the world today with your quick thinking.* And a third person perspective is like someone witnessing what happens. *Drew saved the world today with his quick thinking.*

With your customers, I recommend a first-person story whenever possible. After all, this is your story. A third-party example can work if your personal life doesn't provide an applicable case, but third-party stories are always inherently weaker than using something that happened to you. Oprah Winfrey's speech that we saw earlier is a good example of a personal illustration.

Looking back through this book, you will notice several **personal illustrations**. My original story about growing up on the farm and learning from my Papaw was a personal illustration. My story about the birth of my daughter and my subsequent battle with cancer was also a personal illustration. My *purpose* was to demonstrate vulnerability and create a connection with you, the reader by being genuine and real with my life. I'm not sure if it worked with you or not as you read those stories, but it generally works extremely well in front of a live audience. The key to these types of stories isn't just that I'm open to being vulnerable but that I'm genuinely interested in connecting with you. If you tell stories to manipulate your audience, you will never connect on a lasting level that garners true trust and partnership.

Using Metaphors and Similes

The second technique is use of a *metaphor*. This is a literary figure of speech that compares *unrelated* things or concepts to make a point. A metaphor uses one thing to mean another.

Abraham Lincoln, accepting his party's nomination to run for the U.S. Senate seat in Illinois, tackled the critical problem of slavery in The United States by comparing the nation to a house:

"A house divided against itself cannot stand. I believe this government cannot endure, permanently, half slave and half free . . . I do not expect the house to fall, but I do expect it will cease to be divided. It will become all one thing or all the other."[20]

Lincoln, of course, got this metaphor from the Bible (Mark 3:25), but in either case—Jesus or Lincoln—the point was to use the visual image of a building (a house) to represent in Jesus's case the loyalty of His followers and in Lincoln's case The United States with its slave and free states.

We use metaphors all the time: "it's raining cats and dogs," "all the world's a stage," "purple haze, all in my brain," or "knock his block off." Let's go back to Mr. Miagi when he said: "Walk down right side of road, ok. Walk down left side of road, ok. Walk down middle of road, get squished like grape." He was speaking of the need for commitment and focus, not interstate travel!

Remember the Billy Graham speech from earlier? What did he use? A metaphor: "Let's check the stitches." Ronald Reagan frequently told a story of a boy on Christmas morning who went outside and saw a four-foot high pile of mulch and manure. He began digging. His horrified parents came out and said, "What are you doing!!?" He said, "With this much manure there has to be a pony in here somewhere."

A *simile* is similar to a metaphor, and is in fact a specific kind of metaphor, but uses "like," "as," or "such as" to make a clear point of comparison. "She disappeared like the wind." "This steak is as tough as leather." Usually, metaphors are meant to enhance your communication, not to particularly make a serious point as Lincoln did with the "house divided" or "What's down in the well comes up in the bucket."

Using Analogies

A third technique, closely related to the use of metaphor and simile, is the use of an **analogy**. Analogies may use metaphors and similes to make comparisons, except that they aren't always figures of speech or merely simple comparisons (like "I'm as hungry as a horse"); rather they are logical arguments that relate things that are otherwise not similar. "The brain is a super-powerful computer."

"Just as a warrior's sword is his weapon, the writer's weapon is his words." "Country music is to him what sunlight is to a vampire!" Or as Carl Sanburg said, "Life is like an onion: You peel it off one layer at a time, and sometimes you weep."

My son, Drew, has a severe peanut allergy. It's severe enough that he can go into anaphylaxis and potentially be in a life-threatening situation if he's exposed to or ingests peanuts. Our local school district has been great in most aspects of our kids' educational (albeit mostly left-brained) needs. When it comes to Drew's allergy, we meet every year before the first day of school to go over how to handle his allergy with the new teacher and all the supportive staff. Now, a rational person would just assume that with so many kids having this allergy these days, why wouldn't it just be a "peanut free" school. No such luck.

As the meeting unfolded, we were not getting the level of detail around the "program" to protect our son that we were hoping for. My wife was getting visibly upset to the point of tears when she fell silent for a few seconds, and then looked up at the staff and simply asked, "Would you be ok if a child brought a loaded gun into this school?"

There were a few curious looks and you could tell they weren't quite sure how to respond when my wife continued, "Letting my son get near peanut products poses the same danger as someone pointing a loaded gun." It was a powerful analogy, and it had a powerful impact. The defensive tone of the staff changed instantly and we had their full cooperation from that point forward. You go, story-based girl!

Warren Buffet communicates all the time in analogies and metaphors. Here's one of my favorite Mr. B quotes where he's communicating the difference between a seasoned investor versus someone simply getting lucky: "A strong market is like a high tide: everyone can make money, but it's only when the tide goes out that you discover who's been swimming naked."

Using Visual Aids or a Prop

The final technique is a *Visual aid* or *Prop*. Those of you old enough to remember presidential candidate Ross H. Perot recall that in the 1992 campaign for president, Perot constantly used simple charts to show the nation's debt or spending levels. (He also was fond of metaphors. When referring to the economy, he would tell talk show host Larry King, "Larry, we just gotta get under the hood and fix it.")

In 2012 Israeli Prime Minister Benjamin Netanyahu spoke to the United Nations about the danger of Iran obtaining a nuclear weapon. He used a picture of an old-fashioned "Stratego"-type bomb, with the different levels marked off showing how far Iran had come. The last level, he said, was the one we were now in, where the "bomb" could "explode" at any minute.

If your product is small enough, there is no substitute for *holding* something physically in front of people. The tangibility of showing people the product in your hand is powerful. I knew an author who had a book that did reasonably well, but he got on a national television show and the host repeatedly held up the copy of the book and showed it to audiences. Boom! His sales went straight to the *New York Times* best-seller list. Of course it helps if the host has more than five viewers, but even then, I bet he would have sold five books!

If you have a product or service that can be displayed easily, and demonstrated or performed effortlessly, this will be a particularly effective tool for you, but *only* after you have made the connection through a story. It's useful to remember that to be viewed as a master of your product, service or craft, a powerful way to get your customer to visualize benefits is through an interactive demonstration. Allowing your customers to see, touch, and feel your product is like being sucked into a movie. They immediately become the main character and see how the product or service will *actually* benefit them.

So, to review, our four techniques to tell a story are:

Personal Illustration
Metaphor
Analogy/Simile
Visual aid or prop

Let's see if we can wind all four together. You meet a potential client. After the obligatory introduction, perhaps you pull a gold coin out of your pocket.

"You know, my dad gave me this when I turned sixteen. He said, 'Son, this is your future!' I first thought he meant that making money was the key to success, but later I overheard him in a business conversation. He had made a deal that had lost money, and had lingering debts as a result. He told his associate, "It doesn't matter that the company owed you that money. *I made the promise*, and I'll make sure you get every dime that is owed to you. It may take a while, but I will make sure you get repaid!" When he saw me, he winked and pulled out a gold coin of his own from his pocket. Then I got it. The coin was like his word—it was honor, it was trust. It was like he could read my mind. You wanted your future to rest on the confidence people had that you would do what you said you would do."

Do we need to break that down? First, mentioning *my dad gave me this when I turned sixteen* makes this a **personal illustration**. Second, by using a coin, the story involved a ***visual aid—a prop***. Third, the story used a *metaphor*: trust is gold. Yet the story never lost sight of the thing people always connect with the most: values, connection, trust. Who wouldn't want their reputation to be sterling, except maybe the Grinch or Gru from *Despicable Me*!

When I teach these techniques in seminars, I have participants build a story lifeline. First, early in the day, I have them each tell a story—usually about a time in their life when they overcame a significant obstacle. Later, I ask them to identify the **Five Elements** of the stories they told earlier that day. They then write this down, and analyze what elements their story may have missed. Without fail, the stories that have the most connection with their peers closely follow the Story Lifeline.

Let's go back now and see how the two stories I told you earlier follow the **Five Elements** and how to apply the **Four Techniques** to each.

In the earlier relation-focused story about my cancer, the *Purpose* was to create trust and relate-ability. I attempted to do that through a *Personal Illustration*. My initial goal was to create a *Connection* with the reader as early as possible. I did that by describing the fact that I was newly married and wanted to have a family. Most people can certainly connect with this. I gave even more visual details by describing holding my daughter in my trembling arms. I introduced the first *Barrier* in the form of "fear." It was my fear of not knowing how to be a dad, of worrying about not being able to provide or protect her. Many dads (and moms) have that fear and so this serves to further connect the listener.

The big *Barrier* then comes in the form of my cancer. The *Aha Factor* is when you realize that I was able to overcome the cancer, defeat my fear of not being there for my wife and daughter, and have the courage to fight for *them*. The *Resolution* was that the listener/reader could imagine the hardest things they are currently dealing with or have dealt with at some point in their life, and the perspective of how they too overcame or are now encouraged to make it through their current situation.

You can't hear a story like that and not *feel* something. It might provoke a thought, but you will quickly notice how that thought turned into a feeling. What is born from a story like that? Trust. It's hard not to trust someone who believes what you believe about life, and my guess is that most of you reading this *believe* that family is important and *believe* that the human spirit can overcome the greatest of obstacles with enough faith and perseverance.

So, in summary, this was a **Relation-Focused Story** that followed the **Purpose-Connection-Barrier/Conflict-Aha Factor-Resolution** Story Lifeline and used a **Personal Illustration** as the primary delivery technique. (You will also notice a few metaphors and analogies sprinkled in as well.)

So, how do you apply this to *persuasion-focused* stories? You have to establish a connection that allows the customer to see himself in that situation. What is his barrier, and how does he overcome it?

You can do the same exact exercise with "Martha's" story to see if you can take the "persuasion-focused" story and align it to the Story Lifeline as well as pick out the techniques employed in the story. Over time, you will actually be able to listen to any story and recognize the flow of the lifeline. Many times, you will notice that it is missing an element or two. You will also notice that you likely didn't connect quite as well with those stories missing one or more of the five elements.

This is very much the Mr. Miagi "wax on/wax off" approach, in that the elements might not seem all that impressive individually, but when they are all put together you have Daniel-san. This process is very much a story lifeline that continues from call to call, not an "arc" that returns you to the bottom at the end. Your next visit should build upon the previous relationship of trust and grow upward from there.

Sometimes the technique doesn't get the resolution you want. Netanyahu wanted support to stop Iran from getting a nuke. The "aha" was that Israel didn't want to do it alone. But there has been no resolution yet.

Papaw used to say, "Never tell a story without a point; never make a point without a story." If you don't stick to the lifeline, you may never get to your point. You have to be succinct. "Brevity is the soul of wit."

> "Never tell a story without a point. Never make a point without a story."
> —WILLIE "PAPAW" BLOOMFIELD

You need to develop a "bank" of two-to-three relation-focused and persuasion-focused stories. Make sure you're using a balance of the four techniques (personal illustrations, metaphors, analogies/similes, and visual aids) and make sure your stories follow the story lifeline. Over time, you will become better and better at creating stories on the fly, in the moment, that are perfect for that specific listener. Until such time, it's good to have a few "go-to" stories to share when the anxiety kicks in and the stress takes over.

There is a larger purpose occurring while you are going through the narrative—called the "big story." Think about a family vacation. More specifically, think about *National Lampoon's Vacation.* The purpose was to get away as a family. Chevy Chase going to Wally World, but there are sub-stories from Aunt Edna, to Cousin Eddie, to Christie Brinkley trying to seduce Clark Griswold. If you don't get this reference, you are either really young or have some homework to do once you finish reading this book. If those sub-stories follow the Story Lifeline consistently, they help build the larger narrative more effectively.

How you get your customer to Wally World is the result of how effective you use the stories. You want your customer to go to Wally World *with* you, so you may have to tell a story just to get him in the Family Truckster!

Next, see if you can tell your company's story utilizing SBS techniques. Try to follow the Story Lifeline as well as you possibly can. The key is to allow your company to take on almost "human" characteristics. That's how your customer will relate. Instead of simply reading your annual report, line by line or the "about us" tab on your website, try something a bit different. Let's look at a before SBS and after SBS company story example.

Before:

Mr. Jones, I'm not sure if you're familiar with my company, Sellulots, Inc. We were founded in 1985 by James Lots. We grew from 15 employees to the 2000 we have today. We went public in 1995 and today our stock trades at $100 per share. We first introduced our flagship product, Compuclean in 1990 and it is now the #1 corporate security software in the U.S.A. We have over 50,000 customers and a strong reputation for service. Would you like to be customer 50,001?

How many of you are reading this and thinking, "I never tell my company story like that!!" I bet it's not too far off—is it, really? When you tell your company story, always be mindful of the lingering question in the back of your customer's mind every step of the way: **"So what!"** Re-read the story above now from the perspective of the customer and ask "So what?" after each point. Do you see it now? No connection. Left-brained. Let's try it a different way:

After:

Mr. Jones, I loved reading the story of your company on your website. I can't believe you started this company back in 1980 in your basement with $500 and a rotary dial phone. Amazing. I'm not sure if you realized it or not, but our founder, James Lots, founded Sellulots in a very similar way. He began in the warehouse of his father's shipping company with a desk in the corner, no capital and a hand me down desktop computer. His first year was extremely difficult. What was that first year like for you?

(You've already connected by a comparative "beginnings" story so getting him to tell more here will be engaging and informative.)

"That is quite a first year! What's interesting is how your story meshes so well with the reason Mr. Lots created our flagship product, Compuclean. He often tells the story of how small businesses like yours had constant problems with security breaches to their networks that cost them millions. His solution quickly made him the best friend of every small to medium sized business in Cincinnati. Well, it looks like you've grown tremendously since those early days. Good news is, so have we. Can you tell me how you handle your company's security infrastructure today?"

Now, this is simply telling your company story using an illustration and leveraging the customer's story as well. I could have just as easily used a "parallel analogy" where I compare our company's story to something the customer is familiar with. This exercise is extremely difficult to communicate with clarity in print, but in our workshops the light bulb comes on quickly. The point is, as long as you are utilizing the SBS techniques, asking great questions to get their story out, and keeping the interaction in the right brain, you are heading for connection.

When it comes to barriers/conflict/tension in a story, most of us are drawn to these intuitively, but likely have never dissected our stories to see just how integral they are to the story's effectiveness. From *Winnie the Pooh* to *Pulp Fiction*, you do not have a story without conflict. I would love if Story-Based Selling could guarantee you great success without facing difficulty, but that would be the greatest lie written in a book since the serpent deceived Adam and Eve in the Garden of Eden.

While that may be more than a tad overstated, it shows that conflict is nothing new. It is also nothing unique. Nothing unites people like a common enemy, and if you are listening to a story, chances are you will be drawn in and feel a part of the action.

What happens when we all root together? Suddenly there is home-field advantage and a bond formed. Just like we can hug a total stranger when our team scores a game-winning touchdown, we celebrate overcoming trials because of this connection.

Who didn't cheer at the end of *The Shawshank Redemption*? Andy Dufresne faced extreme conflict, from an unjustified imprisonment to being brutally beaten; we felt for him every step of the way. Even though most of us are not facing these same difficulties, at least I certainly hope not, we all identify with someone who has been treated unfairly. We all identify with someone who has been kicked when he is down. We all want that happy ending, especially when it seems so unlikely.

What kind of story do you have if your characters are Mr. Perfect and Mrs. Perfect who live on Utopia Boulevard with their children Ideal and Angelic and their new perfectly house-trained puppy? Sure, it sounds nice, but it is not exactly relatable.

If you come to someone with something that is too perfect, both the right and left brain sound alarms and unite in delivering a rejection. The same goes for your story. Do not be afraid of conflict while thinking it is going to create a messy picture because people relate to messy pictures. They also relate to obstacles and objections.

The point I am making here is simple: real is better than perfect. Give people something real to cheer for. Give them something recognizable to overcome. This is where people start relating to you. This is how a connection is formed.

> "Conflict cannot survive without your participation."
> —WAYNE DYER
> Best-selling author of self-help books and popular motivational speaker

In summary, the SBS Categories, Elements, and Techniques work as your tools to create your Story Lifeline. Over time, you will find that you don't have to "paint the fence" or "wax on or off" any longer and the story building process will become natural. I can't tell you how many times in the middle of a workshop a participant throws out a question and asks what "technique" I would use. Usually, some random analogy or personal illustration comes flowing to my mind as if I've told it a million times. What I try to explain to them in that moment is that success with these tools comes over time, not in two days. I have become so used to speaking in story form that everything is a story to me. It's now second nature. It will be the same for you, too. It just takes a bit of practice, discipline and coaching. Pretty much like everything else in life, huh?

WHAT'S *YOUR* STORY?

❋ *Which are harder for you to develop, Relation-Focused or Persuasion-Focused stories?*

❋ *How well can you tell your company's story today?*

❋ *When you reflect on a story you've recently told or have recently heard, did it follow the Story Lifeline? Which elements were missing?*

❋ *When you think of the four SBS techniques, how can you leverage each in your story? Your company's story?*

❋ *Try to tell your company's story using only a parallel analogy. It may seem hard at first, but becomes much easier with time.*

4

The Concept of Empathetic Active Listening

"You're short on ears and long on mouth!"
—JOHN WAYNE, *Big Jake,* 1971

You are now armed with the most important information on how to improve your communications, namely the art of the story. But before you tell your story or your company's story, remember that you need to engage your client in the right brain with insightful, opening questions. I won't spend any time here discussing what questions you should ask; let's just say they need to be open-ended and visually focused for the customer. From there, you must develop the skill that most salespeople are lacking—even above communicating in story form—and that is listening.

Do Ya *Feel* Me?

How do we actively engage people in such a way as we move the conversation immediately into the right brain? You know the answer: leverage SBS techniques and then get them to tell their story. But if you can't listen, and listen effectively, this will prove difficult. From the moment we open our mouth until the time we walk out of the office, if a person starts with a left-brain approach, it is very difficult to get the customer back to right brain. And remember: our habit, our practice, is to immediately go into "data dump mode." Your first left-brain inclination is to *explain* the value of your product and to hit the customer or client with a blizzard of "whys." Why he or she should use your service, hire you, adopt your processes, etc.

Overcoming this all begins with listening and understanding your client's needs, and not just the immediate "problem" you will "solve," but the long-term goals that you will address to form a relationship. And this starts with active listening techniques, which not only get the discussion into a right-brain context, but helps you make sense of the customer's story.

Everyone wants people to empathize with them, but not sympathize for them. Stephen Covey observed, "Most people do not listen with the intent to understand; they listen with the intent to reply." True dat.

Salespeople will ask about the customer's job, or product, or business, but they already have a pre-programmed response as to how they expect the answers to come back. In most cases, they are planning their answer the *entire time the client is offering his response!* As we have seen, salespeople walk into a call and begin to "data dump," which goes back to how they were educated to memorize numbers, facts, and figures. Active listening is quite different. It involves getting a person talking about his or her business and then listening for the elements of storytelling to try to fit them in your story lifeline. In particular, this will allow you to identify the barrier points and the "pain points" of the story. When you know that, you can help address the solution.

> "Wisdom is the reward you get for a lifetime of listening when you'd have preferred to talk."
> —DOUG LARSON
> *The Far Side*

One approach is to avoid asking about the reason you were brought there, even if you think you know the "problem" that needs to be "solved." Instead, ask general questions about the business—strategy, vision, and direction.

Have you ever called someone expecting to get his or her voice mail, and then they surprise you by answering the phone? It throws you off. Your left brain is ready to deliver information, when all of a sudden it feels like it has a bad connection. You are now discombobulated by something foreign like human contact.

Chances are, you will face some of these awkward moments as you transition to a Story-Based Selling philosophy. You have all the data, but the system has changed and you may not know how to deliver it. This throws you off because you were not ready to listen. Many of us need to switch gears and downshift into listening mode. In this mode you are not just listening for information, but rather for what this person is really trying to relate to you. We have all heard the expression, "It's all about what is left unsaid." This is your job here.

Active listening involves more than just the ability to recite information. Remember how we talked about tone and body language before? In active listening you will be able to pick up on more than you knew you were looking for.

Don't worry; as I said, this takes time and practice. It also takes listening and a little patience. These are good things, albeit often unpopular, but it will pay off, no matter your field.

**"One of the most sincere forms of respect is
actually listening to what another has to say."**
—BRYANT H. MCGILL, *Voice of Reason*

Once you are at this point, you are ready for the next step, which is to: *listen for buying signals*—key phrases and key words that signal either willingness to move forward or an objection to the product. The goal is to get you to listen to the world around you, and get you to communicate and think in story form.

Throughout, you want to *clarify*. Clarification is an active listening technique. It is not *parroting*, but when you first start it may come across that way. You draw an analogy rather than repeating, so that you understand.

Let's say you are selling a couch to a woman with three kids less than five years old. Your store is full of furniture ranging from fine and delicate to durable. Just by having the children in tow, she has shared what her needs are. At this point you can talk about warranty, thread counts, and stain resistance all you want, but if you share that a certain model is "the closest thing to toddler-proof I have ever seen," you have her attention.

This opens the door for your own story. You are free to talk about the time your daughter created some performance art with a chair and glass of purple Kool-Aid, or your son who used the ottoman to perfect his somersault, but the ER doctor suggested he quit the sport. If you have pets or a sloppy brother-in-law, tell that story. You have stories and so does she. Therefore she may likely relate to an anecdote about a couch that got a jelly stain on it seconds after you were able to maneuver it through the door.

You don't want to respond with left-brain replies that drive the person back to a left-brain discussion. This leads to a back and forth scenario akin to an argument. I had an uncle tell me once, "Figures don't lie, but liars can figure." Why does this ring so true? Because it shows an inherent distrust we all live with. Facts and figures are scrutinized a lot more thoroughly than a story. It is also a lot more difficult to relate to a number than a person. Do not make yourself less relatable; share a little of yourself and see what happens.

Remember what part of the brain stamps the approval. The right brain handles the connections, while the left brain tackles the transactions. Which one sounds like a more pleasant conversation? We are not even talking about overcoming opposition because we are not there yet. Sometimes you never get there because you won't have to.

If you want to explain this to the left hemisphere, just label this as handling a "no" before it happens. This also will decrease the amount of stress you put on yourself. Are we talking high-pressure selling here? Certainly not; rather we are sharing a bit of ourselves, and inviting the customer to do the same.

Is this your first thought when it comes to sales? It definitely does not fit the stereotype. Some people may think Story-Based

Selling should have the tag line: *It's not your grandfather's sales.* But for me, it certainly is because he is the one who taught me to tell a story in the first place.

What is another prized characteristic of a good salesperson? Most people would likely say they must have a strong knowledge of the product. And yes, this certainly is important. I remember a time at a hardware store when a salesperson "helping me" did not know the difference between a nut and a bolt. I am going with the assumption that if you are in the field, you do actually know what it is that you are selling. Most organizations today do a great job of teaching you the "what" but few even attempt to help you tackle the "how."

But, do you know your customer? Do you know what their needs are? Do you know what makes them tick? Since most people do not walk around with a laminated demographic sheet detailing all their information, you have to get their story out somehow.

A story gives you all the information in a much more tangible package. Chances are, if you're listening, you will also find they will tell you so much more than *they* even realize. If you, yourself, get hung up hearing only facts and figures, you will never hear the customer's story in the depth necessary to ask appropriate right-brained questions.

We need to be mindful of how we ask these follow-up questions to keep the interaction in the right brain. Closed-ended questions here are a connection killer. Instead, ask a question that you would ask someone you are not selling to. Granted, yes, we have already discussed that everyone is trying to sell something. In this case though, do not think about the dollars and cents that will follow. Do not let the left brain sabotage the connection you have just made.

Follow up with a question you would ask a friend. You would likely listen to a friend differently than you would a salesperson calling on you, and perhaps that is part of the problem. Maybe a question along the lines of, "Boy, I can see how the layoffs have put extra pressure on you and your team. How are you personally feeling about all these changes?" You will likely get a more detailed story. A right-brained story involving her *"feelings"* about the changes. If you listen with the intent to understand, you will likely hear many areas of opportunity for you to come to the rescue.

Please note that we are talking active listening, not *selective* hearing. You will learn so much more about people if you practice active listening. People will be drawn to you because everyone wants to be heard. This is not in-depth philosophy, it is a basic human need. Active listening brings an audience just as effectively as speaking does. This may not make immediate sense, but think about it; you are inviting an audience that is giving back to you. Active listening attracts the crowd you need to know.

Planning Your First Impression

Remember, so much of this hinges on a first impression, and you'll only have seconds to make a first impression, so, how do you engage immediately? This will take some practice, and some forethought. You should develop unique and original ways of introducing yourself, perhaps through analogy or self-deprecation.

Remember how President Ronald Reagan used to frequently dispel questions about his age? He would use self-deprecating humor, such as when he said, "Thomas Jefferson once said, 'We should never judge a president by his age, only by his works.' And ever since he told me that, I stopped worrying." Or, "I have left orders to be awakened at any time in case of national emergency, even if I'm in a cabinet meeting." Then there was this famous quip during his debate with Jimmy Carter: "I am not going to exploit, for political purposes, my opponent's youth and inexperience."

Groucho Marx famously said, "I wouldn't want to be a member of any club that would have someone like me as a member." You don't want to lay it on too thick, but just enough to put the client at ease.

While speaking of humor, why do so many speeches open up with a joke? This is to start off by relating to the audience. If a speaker starts off a presentation with an onslaught of facts and figures, where does the audience go? Bye-bye to left-brain land.

I know we have been trained to uncover "need" and "pain" and if we're not careful, our line of questioning can come across to our customers as leading or manipulative. I had a moment of clarity in a workshop a while back. The class went down a rabbit trail for a few minutes bantering back and forth with each other about the best way to make the customer think you really care about them. Their intentions were pure, but it smacked of the manipulation "vibe" that I try to obliterate with this program.

Finally, one of the participants asked me what I thought was the best way to make the customer think you care about them. Without really thinking, I responded, "Do you really want to know the #1 secret to making a customer think you care about them?" My response, "You *actually* have to care about them." There is no substitute. Caring means that you don't approach a customer as the next commission check. Rather, you have to be willing to invest time in learning the inner workings, goals, and processes of the company.

Effective communication also involves the art of silence: When you ask a question, generally someone answers with brevity. Teachers know that when you ask a question, it may be thirty to forty-five seconds before a student will answer, but eventually the student will answer. If you respond with silence, the customer will almost always come back in with more information.

Silence can lead to discomfort, but I attribute that to the belief that so many of us have that someone needs to fill the empty space with talking. We are trying to distance ourselves from the fast-talking salesman. That is a well-established stereotype, but what about the patient salesperson. That certainly is not a common figure, so that in itself can set you apart.

> **"Listening to people keeps them entertained."**
> —MASON COOLEY
> *City Aphorisms,*
> *Eleventh Selections, 1993*

There is an old, unattributed saying, "Silence is often misinterpreted, but never misquoted." Silence is not a bad thing; it's just not overly common. Sometimes your mouth needs a break. Sometimes it takes just a little time to get the answer you seek.

Once you get your answer, you may need to dig deeper. "What's your biggest challenge as vice president of Inventory Management Co.?" The response might be "We're not getting the inventory off the shelf in time." But that doesn't get to the real problem—that Joe down in shipping is not doing the job. Most people selling software will say, "That's interesting, because our software will handle just that problem." But in fact, the software isn't addressing the issue of Joe down in shipping!

One way to get to these deeper answers is through the afore-mentioned open-ended questions. Amateur salespeople ask closed-ended questions that permit the client to respond with one or two words, but trained personnel know to ask open-ended questions. For example, "Explain to me the benefits of an open-ended question," will get you more information than "Does that make sense to you?" The first elicits a longer, more thoughtful response.

In writing this book, do you know how tempting it is to shape my story so that I look like Superman? It would certainly be good for the ego, but you would see through the facade. The simple truth here is that people relate to Clark Kent, not Superman. That's because very few of you reading this are faster than a speeding bullet or can leap over a building, but we have all had times where we felt unprepared and insecure, sometimes due to our own bumbling selves. Here's a Clark Kent moment from my illustrative sales career.

As I mentioned earlier, part of my sales career was dedicated to marketing a drug for lung cancer. One beautiful spring day, I went to my appointment at a local oncology office. I was scheduled to meet with the nurses first, followed by the doctors to give them updates on our drug. I was meeting with the nurses in the break room where they slowly trickled in, grabbed their lunch and sat to hear whatever "schpeel" I was dishing. I knew a few of the key nurses from previous meetings, but there were a few that I didn't.

In my suave, super cool, story-based way I went nurse by nurse finding connecting points and hearing about their day or their family or what have you. I always started with a thought-provoking question that seemed to get them talking. When it came to nurse Betty, for whatever reason, I drew a mental blank and committed the verbal crime above all crimes. I asked her when the baby was due. Now, in all fairness, I had overheard her and another nurse talking about a baby shower and decorating a nursery, etc., so I wasn't just pulling the question out of thin air.

As you may have guessed, the baby shower in question wasn't for the "above the healthy weight limit for her height" nurse Betty. It was for her cousin. Betty wasn't pregnant. The awkward silence in the room was only broken when a different nurse, one much thinner than Betty, interjected with, "Hey, all is not lost. I just found out that I am pregnant!" The room broke out with laughter, but I was clearly sick to my stomach and in an unrecoverable relational pitfall with Betty and who knows how many other nurses!

Needless to say, I did eventually recover and it became a bit of a joke around the office when I would come in. Looking back on it now, most of the staff actually felt sorry for me. They knew I was a stand-up guy who meant well and really cared about people. They also knew they, too, had said things in their lives that they wish they could take back. It actually created a connection point. Even your own stupidity can be a story-based asset, though I wouldn't make a habit of demonstrating it often!

**"Failure is simply the opportunity
to begin again, this time more intelligently."**
—HENRY FORD, *My Life and Work*

What about the person who has certain quasi-superstitious or stereotypical attitudes: ("If you didn't go to the University of Michigan, you are worthless.") We all know in that specific example that person is hopeless and should be ruthlessly insulted. (I grew up a Buckeye. I know what I'm talking about). In those cases, you have to establish a human basis for the relationship. At least you know something he is passionate about, and with that there is a beginning. Since every story has a beginning, you are already underway.

Another thing most stories have is a villain. You know his hero, and if you have any knowledge of sports rivalries, you know Ohio State is on his axis of evil. Agree, disagree, or indifferent, it can be fun to play along, at least for a little while.

There are also differences in the regional cultures of the United States. (Globally as well, but for now we will stick to the USA) I've had the privilege in my career to work with or manage people from all over the country. What I've observed is that the various cultural differences are real and need to be acknowledged and appreciated when working in that geography, but they don't change the impact of the Story-Based Selling philosophy.

A few years back, I managed a sales rep who worked for me in the Greater New York/Manhattan area. The overall pace of communication there was (and still is) incredible. Everyone seemed to be on speed to this country boy. When they talked to each other, it was as if two machine guns were blasting out as many words in as short a time span as possible. I could see how hard it was to "connect" with customers in this region. The reality was they got a tremendous amount of work done in a short period of time, but lacked a feeling of real connection and partnership.

On one particular visit, my sales rep noticed a picture on the wall of what looked like the customer's son and father at Coney Island. He asked a simple question. "When was the last time the three of you have had a chance to do that again?" The customer stopped in their fast paced tracks, looked up at the picture and launched into an emotional story of how her father has passed away just months after that picture. She told us how the three of them had gone to Coney Island every summer since her son had been born. She became emotional and apologized.

My rep did the exact thing I was hoping he would do. He quietly and attentively *listened*. After a few tears and a brief pause, he shared a similar story about his father and his kids. As a silent observer, I could see the connection shoot up like a rocket, clear off the charts.

I sat back against the wall and watched in amazement at how the customer who earlier had only two minutes for us gave us forty-five. She ended up scheduling a dinner with my rep for the following weekend and became one of our best customers. Once we are able to actually tap into a subject that is emotionally moving to them, you can almost feel the world slow down a bit, even if for only a few minutes.

It proves the fact that even fast-paced, hard driving customers in the Northeast still crave connection and still make decisions based on emotion. I could tell you very similar stories from the South and the West of our country as well. They all have unique cultures filled with unique people but in the end, we are all craving connection.

WHAT'S *YOUR* STORY?

* *Do you keep embarrassing stories to yourself for fear of further embarrassment or do you share them to be more relatable?*

* *Do you listen or wait to talk?*

* *What happens when you are not connecting with a customer? What can you do to fix it?*

* *How much time do you spend empathizing with people? Do you listen before trying to offer solutions?*

* *How do you handle silence?*

5

Overcoming Objections with SBS

"The Truth? You Can't Handle the Truth!"
—COLONEL JESSUP, *A Few Good Men*

You don't have to be in the sales force very long to know you are going to face objections. In fact, believe it or not, sometimes people are going to tell you "no." If you're good, you hear it a lot. If you're great, you probably hear it even more.

Then what do you do when faced with such unthinkable rejection? If you are like most people, you look for an immediate rebuttal. More likely than not, you are looking to respond with logic. You know your product is better, and you know why your product is better. Therefore you are programmed to toss out any number of facts why.

Makes sense, right? Doesn't it only stand to reason?

We have all been trained in various "objection handling" models over the years from LAARC (Listen, Acknowledge, Assess, Respond, Confirm) to LACE (Listen, Accept, Commit, Explicit Action) to LAIR (Listen, Acknowledge, Identify Objection, Reverse It) to the trusty ole' "Feel-Felt-Found" method. What do these models all have in common? They are a left-brain attempt to better position the sales person to essentially regurgitate the same data and statistics that caused the objection in the first place.

Our instincts whenever we hear an objection are to "convince" to overcome. How are we trained to convince? With facts. Here's what our customers are hearing sub-consciously when we respond this way, "Mr. Customer, either you were not listening to me a few minutes ago or you are clearly just too stupid to understand what I said. Let me go ahead and repeat myself for the third time with all the features and benefits of our greatness and maybe *then* you will get a clue." I know it may sound like complete hyperbole, but the reality is, it's not far from the actual truth of how we make the customer *feel*. Remember, statistics and facts make them "think" but decisions are made on "feelings" and "emotion." The great poet and actress Maya Angelou once said, "People will forget what you said and people will forget what you did, but people will never forget how you made them *feel*."

For as strange as it may sound, reason and logic do not steer the ship. They keep the ship running efficiently, but at this point they are not calling the shots. This could be why Captain Kirk was at the helm of the ship, and Mister Spock was first officer.

The point here is that your customers are not swayed by logic. They may not know this, but the funny thing here is that most salespeople don't either.

Let's say you are selling laptops. And, just for fun, let's just say your customer knows as much, if not more, about computers as you do. This could make for a very stressful situation. He has more facts, he has more experience, and therefore he has a clear-cut advantage. Right? Not necessarily. In fact, not at all if you follow this philosophy.

You only lose if you turn it into a "me versus him" scenario. At his first objection, you are likely to retort with a "limbic left-brain hook" about processing speed, memory, functionality, and price. Then he may come back with an argument about compatibility, and by the time you counter with superior warranty and twenty-four hour customer service, you lost him and you lost the sale. In fact, you never even had the chance.

At this point you'll probably ask why, especially because you thought you had done everything right. In some regards, you did. You were well in tune with the product, but not the user. Your customer then walks out the door with more knowledge about the laptop, but something unfortunate happens along the way. He does not like you *and* he applies those same *feelings* towards your company.

**"Nothing will ever be attempted if
all possible objections must first be overcome."**
—SAMUEL JOHNSON, *The History of Rasselas, Prince of Abissinia*

I could be talking to a diabetic needing insulin, and they would not buy from me, even if their life depended on it. Communication and relationships are more important than any of us truly understand.

So let's take another look at the laptop scenario. You have a well-informed consumer who is looking for a reason to tell you "no." He's also looking for something else though, and what he's seeking is something in the right-brain wheelhouse. He wants his story told. Therefore, instead of a retort, ask him what that story is. Ask him what brought him into your store in the first place. What is he trying to accomplish with this computer? Is he writing a book, creating a website, playing online games, or connecting with friends?

See, his response to you here is far less likely to involve him walking out the door. Instead, he is going to tell you all about his plans. In fact, within just a few minutes you are likely to hear all about his dreams, his friends, and his favorite games. This is where active listening becomes your greatest asset. Ask him how long he has been working on this dream, where he met these friends, and what his level is on the game.

Remember that scenario of debating facts? Which sounds better? Which is more likely to yield a sale? How about repeat sales?

He was not looking for someone to be an expert for him. He probably did not even think you were interested. You did not know him, and with the old model of answering logically—well, you never would. And speaking of things that would never happen, you never could have had the chance to connect with him.

This is why I love doing what I do. There are over six billion people on this planet. They all have their own story, their own dream. Sales figures and commission checks are a good thing too, don't get me wrong, but along the way I have seen a slice of life from a lot of people I could have just seen as customers.

This is just one example how Story-Based Selling can help you take what is often seen as a negative, and not only turn it into a positive, but make it mutually beneficial. There are cases that may not be as easy, but the same methods still work.

What are the most common obstacles? A handful of these are: price, technology, delivery, and change.

The accountant in all of us has his office on the left side of the brain. So you know where it's coming from when you hear this ever-popular objection, "How much does it cost?" Don't panic, especially if you don't have what you think is the right answer. Sometimes it can be worse if you don't think you have any answer at all. The key to remember when price or cost comes up as an objection is that there is no such thing as an objection to price or cost. What you talkin' about, Willis? In reality, the objection here is always about a lack of perceived *value*, not price. What if we used our newly learned SBS techniques to overcome this objection?

"Mr. Customer, let's say you and I decide to take a trip from New York to San Diego. Of course we want to know how much this trip will cost us, right? Right. Well, before we can get a total cost, we need to ask ourselves a few questions. Are we driving or flying? How many days do we have to get there? Are there any great sights we'd like to see along the way like the Grand Canyon, Yellowstone or even the world's largest ball of string? What type of accommodations are we most interested in, hotels or camping? Motel 6 or Ritz Carlton? What do we want out of this trip and why are we going in the first place?"

Chances are, he won't be expecting these questions. You have just pulled him out of the left-brain, and into the right. Instead of looking at the bottom line, he is now looking at the space between.

"You see, Mr. Customer, I am very in tune with your budget and the overall costs associated with our product but before we get a detailed price, we really need to outline the overall value of the "trip" so we can match our products with your expectations. With that in mind, can I ask you a few more questions around how you'll be using the product and your expectation for implementation?"

Boom. Objection diffused. Customer is now back in the right brain ready for more! In this case, I used the analogy technique but could have just as easily used an illustration, metaphor, or even a visual aid.

Objections about technology and change are often driven by fear. When dealing with fear, how often do you think logic and reason work? How many times have you heard the phrase "irrational fear?" When we are afraid, we feel isolated. When we are isolated we feel that nobody understands us. This is absurd, because I have never met anyone who has never been afraid. Every hero, every champion, has faced some degree of fear. We have all dealt with fear in our lives, and when dealing with someone facing this, the persons need a way to relate. A story is their lifeline here. Someone telling them to not be afraid, quite simply, is not going to work.

Recently my daughter and I were skiing. She is still a novice and had only been on hills above the "bunny" hill once or twice. She had reached the point where she was plenty good enough to ski on the next level hills but on this day, fear was crippling her. After five minutes of me trying to "convince" her that everything would be alright, and trying to give her the "facts" of why she need not be afraid, and how she needed to "buckle down" and face her fears head on, it hit me. It was as if I could see my Papaw standing next to me smiling and whispering, "tell her about the time you went from the beginners hill to the next level."

I began to tell her the story of how her daddy didn't learn to ski until he was in his twenties. I was like a baby giraffe on roller skates. It was quite embarrassing and I fell down every ten seconds. I never made it off the bunny hill the entire day. I was so afraid to go to the next level hill that I almost gave up and went into the lodge. At that point in my story, I just stopped talking. She jumped right in with "What did you do? What happened next???"

I began to tell her how I faced my fear, rode the lift, stood at the top of the next hill, said a little prayer and down I went. I told her how I was scared for about the first fifty feet but then I realized I could do it and even if I fell, I was going to make it down this hill. Once I got to the bottom, it was the most satisfying thing in the world.

She paused, smiled and said, "Let's go to the lift!" We did and she has never looked back. I've always marveled at how people have always treated fear as an enemy that must be vanquished. Fear is actually the greatest ally we have—when we learn how to harness it and use it as fuel. Leveraging fear as a salesperson is no different. It will never be "defeated" so why not saddle it up and ride it! Those who learn how to control their fear have the greatest opportunity for ongoing success. In sales and in life.

When you ask your customers thoughtful questions and then actually listen, you will be amazed how this simple human interaction yields such amazing results. Don't be armed with responses, just listen and be ready with your stories. Humans were created to be social, so when you are talking to someone, it is not simply conversation, but filling a true need.

> "The authentic self is the soul made visible."
> —SARAH BAN Breathnach

What's the lesson here? Be authentic. Ever since the very first salesman tried to sell clubs to help fellow cavemen in their dating life, the profession has been seen in a negative light. The solution is simple. Be real. You have control over your own actions, and you know the right thing to do. Have you ever talked to someone who asked you questions, but had no real interest in your answers? How did this make you feel? Have you ever talked to someone who had all the sincerity of an eviction notice? Would you buy a stick of gum from that person?

As salespeople, we have a tendency to ask questions in order to fill space to give us time to formulate the next thing we will say, regardless if it has anything at all to do with your response! Real objections based on real concerns in the mind of the customer are great. They help move the story forward and allow the customer to strengthen their trust in you and their confidence in your product, assuming you handle those objections with right-brain techniques. Unfortunately, most objections are smokescreens and the customer's invisible "shield" to keep you at a distance and protect themselves from being "sold." Isn't it funny how we all like to buy things but none of us like to be sold?

Please note that Story-Based Selling does not offer a script. It empowers you to grow as a communicator. It equips you to recognize and control fear. The first time I spoke in front of a crowd, I was not able to talk about things like cancer or missing my Pawpaw. I did not know how people would react. I was afraid, so therefore I edited myself. I tried to hold so much control over what others saw that all I allowed them to see was a salesman. If I allowed that to shape my identity, not only would I not be successful in what I do, it would also be miserable and inhibit the emotional connection I get with every workshop I deliver.

When my wife and I were looking to buy our first home, we looked at a lot of houses. We were given a lot of information about square footage, financing, school districts, and resale value. Like most homebuyers, we had someone in our corner. Michael was a good real estate agent. He knew market trends and neighborhoods as well as he knew commission checks. We knew Michael for about three months, but there was something he did not know . . . us.

After the countless houses Michael showed us, we parted ways with him. From there we met Dana. She did not show us a house right away; in fact, she did not seem particularly interested in a sale. Before talking about price she asked about us. She asked about what we'd like to come home to at the end of a long day. She asked about friends and family visiting from out of town, parties, celebrations, and a place to work. Dana also shared her story of buying her first home, frustrations she faced, what attracted her to real estate, and how her twelve-year-old daughter now helps put on open houses. Michael never even asked us if we were dog or cat people, or if we had plans to grow our family. He was prepared to answer our objections and make a sale.

We purchased the third house Dana showed us. Maybe we just felt more at home there right away because she eased our tension. She shared our purpose, which was to simply make a brick structure a home. Even before we walked through the doorway of the first house she initiated the connection by asking about what we were and what we were not looking for. I did not see her as a real estate agent. She had bridged that gap and earned our trust. She did not answer a single question with a dismissive, *Oh don't worry about that.* Buying a house is a long, involved process and the importance of connection cannot be dismissed.

We had that *aha* moment as soon as we walked into what became our home. It was the right choice and met our needs— both right- and left-brained. From the initial offer to the counter, from the financing to the closing, we knew Dana would be there. At no point did we have to look over our shoulder to see if she was still in our corner. She made a strong connection, and that leads to trust, which in turn leads to my family being very happy in a wonderful home.

This serves to show just how strong the right brain is. Most of us will never make a bigger purchase than a house. A place that can require a thirty-year loan comes with a lot of thought, and shouldn't that require some number crunching and analysis? Of course it does, but that is only part of the decision. In the case of our house, the right brain said yes, and the left brain confirmed it.

So how did Dana overcome our objections? She met us where we were, then got to know us better through telling her story, which made us more comfortable to tell our own. I still don't see her as a salesperson, but rather as someone who shared a great experience with us. She knew many of our objections long before we began the active process of looking at houses. She made us comfortable, and any objection we had, we felt free to voice.

An unspoken objection is much more difficult to overcome. It can bite you like a snake you did not know was there. It can also mean that you don't know your customer like you should. There is certainly a vital part of the communication lacking. Also understand that an objection in itself is not a bad thing. Old-school sales training teaches that objections are just another way of saying opportunity. While there is some degree of truth, it goes deeper than that. If you have a connection with your customer, the objection may simply be something you work through. If you do not have that connection, it can be a means to size you up, or perhaps just a reason to say no. Simply stated, if you know your customer, you know their objections.

Sadly, not all salespeople have Dana's approach. We have all run into the cocky salesperson that says ridiculous statements like, "I could sell ice to an Eskimo." Not only is this a turn-off, this mentality skips vital parts of the connection process. For a salesperson, the purpose of each interaction has to be connected to the customer. If there is no purpose, there is no connection. If I am selling consulting services, I'm likely not going to make a sale to a kid buying candy with his allowance money. I could have a great spiel about our unique business tools and substantial ROI, but if I can't offer anything in the way of a Jolly Rancher, then I'm not sharing in his purpose, which certainly shows that my active listening needs work.

Of course that is an extreme example, but if you are not sharing in a purpose, you might as well try to sell business services to a kid buying candy.

Not only does there need to be a connection between the salesperson and the buyer, but there needs to be the connection to the product. Some products sell themselves. How much personal connection does a salesperson need if he's selling a smartphone to a guy who camped out for the three days to buy the new model the day it came out? While this is a pretty easy sale, do not overlook the human element. Even if you know he is going to buy your product, it is still a bad idea to tell him to at least pack some breath mints for his next three-day campout. The buyer-seller relationship should not end with a purchase; it should just be starting.

If you were to stereotype a car salesperson's pitch, you would likely say something like, "What's it going to take to get you in this car today?" What the customer hears is, "How quickly can I get your money?"

Talk about starting off on the wrong foot. Not only is it ineffective; it is almost as insulting as suggesting another breath mint. The customer is not going to like the approach. Therefore the customer will not like the salesperson. It should come as no surprise that the customer is not connected to the product, and any semblance of trust is long gone.

If you were in this situation, would you be able to picture yourself driving this car, even if you were sitting in the driver's seat at the time? Would you see yourself pulling into the driveway or washing it on the weekend? How comfortable would you feel visualizing driving up to the golf course or the grocery store in this new vehicle? Instead, you would be so put off by the pushy sales tactic that the left brain is not going to even run the numbers because the right brain already said no.

Right or wrong, that is going to be the decision that stands. The car may be a great deal. It may be a terrific opportunity, but if that purpose is not shared, there is no connection, the barrier is too great, there is no room for an aha moment, and you do not buy the car. Any objections you would have given would not have been genuine, but rather an excuse to leave in the same car you drove onto the lot.

We have talked a lot about stories, but you may ask why they are effective in dealing with objections. The answer lies in the core of every story: the barrier or conflict. There is some obstacle the protagonist must face and we root for the hero to win. And why do we root for the hero to win? Because we care. People do not generally care about people they do not know, so therefore be known. Put yourself out there. As we talked about before, do not be afraid to be vulnerable. That is what makes people relate to you. Better yet, that is what makes people root for you. The connection you create puts them on your team, and they feel free to leave their anxiety behind. Before you know it, they will care.

This human element stuff does seem to get a little fluffy at times, I admit. I guess that's why we call them "soft skills." But I can tell you from my own experience and the experience of the countless sales professionals I have trained and managed over the years, that the people who actually take the time to care, listen, and engage with their customers are the people who consistently end up on the top of the sales rankings year after year. Objection handling is quite easy when you have trust and a good connection. Add in the SBS techniques and you've got yourself a recipe for accelerated success.

Practice being yourself. How ridiculous does this sound? Perhaps not as much as it initially seems. For years many of us have put on the persona of being what we thought was right. This may take time to unlearn. It takes a degree of courage to be vulnerable. Like anything else, it will take practice. If you have been operating under that persona, your real voice may sound awkward. But it needs to be heard, and not just by your customer.

So what is your story? We discussed this early on, but has your answer changed? Are you less afraid? Fear is crippling, and change is a leading cause of this anxiety, even if it is for the good.

In sales, the spotlight shines on you. If you are like the vast majority out there, your dress rehearsal did you no favors. You trained yourself to battle objections. You trained yourself to win. But then where is your victory? Did you prove you were right? Did you win a battle? Where is your customer in all this?

I hope you now have a few new ideas on how to overcome objections using Story-Based Selling. Like everything else with this methodology, it starts with having a purpose, building connection and joining with the customer on a mutual journey/partnership as opposed to attempting to force them into your epic novel of sales adventure and success. When you write the story together, they become as invested in the stories success as you do. Then you both win.

WHAT'S *YOUR* STORY?

* *How have you been trained to overcome objections in your career?*

* *What are the top three objections you hear on a regular basis?*

* *How can you leverage SBS techniques to overcome those objections?*

* *Think of the last customer that told you no. Why?*

* *How might that conversation look different today if you went back in with SBS techniques?*

6

The Power of Humility, Authenticity, and Vulnerability

"Oh Lord, It's Hard to Be Humble . . ."

—Song by MAC DAVIS

One of my favorite C.S. Lewis quotes of all time is, "Humility is not thinking less of yourself, it's thinking of yourself less." I'm sure every generation feels the generation coming behind them does not fully appreciate or understand all that they have and all that's been done for them. I will say, though, that I am terribly concerned about the entitled, borderline-narcissistic generation that we are in and what's coming up behind us. That's not a prideful judgment on my part, as I see these same flaws in myself. We live in a society that constantly reinforces the need to "get yours" and "do whatever it takes" to get ahead.

I believe the number-one stumbling block in the way of every salesperson can be summed up with a single word: Pride. Most will tell you that to be a great competitor, you need to have that edge. You need that "killer instinct." You can't worry about what other people think. They are only distractions on your way to the top.

What's difficult is I am one of the most competitive people I know. I love to win. I love to compete. I guess I get it honestly. Growing up, basketball was one of my favorite sports. On our farm, we had a gravel driveway. It wasn't the ideal surface for a basketball court, but it's what I had to work with. I took a three quarter-inch piece of plywood, bolted a rim to it, and hung it on the tree at the end of our driveway. I would play for hours, rain or shine.

My dad would occasionally join me in a game of one on one. He refused to let me win. In fact, he was famous for shoving you into the briar patch as you were going up for the game winning shot! If you were to beat the old man, you had to earn it. I grew up fighting and clawing for everything I could. I wanted to be the best athlete, best student, best driver . . . you name it. I cared deeply for other people, but my guess is that no one knew that by my actions.

Why was I so prideful? Why is anyone prideful? Humility means that the hopes, fears, pain, sorrow, delights, and joys of others are as important as our own. Even more important is that we recognize them as such with our actions. Humility means setting aside our own agendas and issues and even for a brief moment to put someone else's first. It means recognizing your own faults as well as the strengths of others. Humility allows us to see our own limitations and allows others to see us as kind, caring, and relatable. We all have flaws but when you try to come across as though you don't, it further alienates you from others. In order to show vulnerability, you must be humble. In order to truly connect with others, you must allow them to see that you recognize your own humanness.

When I share my Papaw story in my live workshops or speaking engagements, I still get emotional. It's real. It's raw. I didn't used to share it in as much detail as I do today. One day in a workshop I was setting up the day and introducing the birth of Story-Based Selling. It's in this section that I share the Papaw story. For whatever reason, on this day I kept going deeper. I continued telling the story even as the emotions of that cold February day came rushing back to me. I tried hard to contain my emotion as I told the story, but on this day, it was meant to be.

> **"Pride makes us artificial and humility makes us real."**
> —THOMAS MERTON
> Trappist monk and author best known for *The Seven Storey Mountain*

What happened was an eye opener for me. When people began sharing their stories that day, many told stories of deep personal relationships—stories that moved many in the room to tears. Showing that level of authenticity and vulnerability allowed everyone to feel okay with doing the same.

I'm certainly not suggesting you lay all your "brain junk" stories at the feet of your customer the first time you meet with them. However, finding a way to show your heart, your passion, and your humility in front of the customer will supercharge your ability to connect.

Most of us are our own biggest obstacles to accomplishing this feat. Don't take yourself so seriously. Remember, people will not relate to you if you are perfect. And since you are not perfect (no offense) do not try to act like it. That persona only leads to distrust.

Why do we root for the underdog? Because we have all experienced setbacks. We have all been knocked down. Would the story of *Rudy* have been as memorable if he was a top-recruit, All-American who dominated the game every time he took the field? No, most people rooted for Rudy because he was like "one of us."

Showing humility removes the separation that can be created with a false pretense. People will see some of themselves in you.

"I had no idea that being your authentic self could make me as rich as I've become. If I had, I'd have done it a lot earlier."
—OPRAH WINFREY, interview with Facebook COO Sheryl Sandberg

Like I said, I am competitive. I like to win. That, of course, has put me in places where I not only lost, but did so with an audience. If you are living out of pride, these losses are devastating. It can seem unfathomable that you are not holding the trophy every time. Humility allows you to see the whole picture and put the loss in perspective. It also gives you the ability to laugh about it, so you are not living with the memory of failure.

James M. Barrie once said, in *The Night Watchers*, "Life is a long lesson in humility." Isn't this true! We are all on a journey, and it's like any adventure—there is opposition. Sometimes there are simple mistakes or misunderstandings. I was horrified when I made that mistake with Nurse Betty, so in that case I guess I had humility thrust upon me. But if I had continued to try and "save face" I would have further embarrassed her, and myself.

The higher you put your own pedestal, the farther you have to fall. We have also talked a little about self-depreciating humor. A subtle joke here and there can show your customer that you do not take yourself too seriously. In turn, they won't either. What happens next is that dividing walls have been taken down, trust is established, and you can now communicate more effectively.

In my life, I have seen that my level of genuine, authentic relationships is in direct proportion to my level of humility. It's been a painful lesson at times, but one worth learning. Now there would be a great irony if I talked at length about how great I am at humility. It's something I stay aware of, and if I stray from it, my stories will quickly remind me. If not, my wife does.

WHAT'S *YOUR* STORY?

* *Do you equate humility with weakness or strength?*

* *Does pride keep you from connecting with your customers?*

* *Think about the last time you could not connect with a customer. What might have bridged the gap?*

* *Do you find yourself competing with your customers?*

* *When do you find people relating to you the most?*

7

The Keys to Change

"I've Got a Little Change In My Pocket..."
—THE GEORGIA SATELLITES

We all know the lines: "The more things change, the more they remain the same." What's more, as we mature, we find this to be increasingly true. The Who, in a song made famous again by the television show *CSI*, sang, "Meet the new boss . . . same as the old boss." Solomon, purported to be the wisest human to ever live, wrote "There is nothing new under the sun." Any Hollywood screenwriter will tell you that all film plots follow one of three time-tested story lines: man against man, man against nature, and man against himself. I'm not sure about you, but I tend to follow the last story line more often than not.

"It's nothing," returned Mrs. Chick.
"It's merely change of weather. We must expect change."
—CHARLES DICKENS, *Dombey and Son*

But there is "change" and there is something called "transformation." Many people have an aversion to "change" because it is often temporary. Think of a diet, quitting smoking, or adopting an exercise routine (the famous "New Year's Resolutions"!). But *transformation* needs to be permanent and can dramatically improve our lives forever. The butterfly is a good analogy. A caterpillar did not just change; it transformed and can never go back to its previous state. If

97

we transform the way we communicate, we will never go back to our previous habits of communication.

My definition of *change* is simply this: to alter or make different; to exchange one for another. On the other hand we define *transformation* as the process of irreversibly altering something or someone to a new or different state. You can change your shoes but your feet are still your feet. You can change your living room furniture, but your house is still your house. You can change your shirt, you can change your job, and you can change nearly anything by swapping it out for something else. Change by itself is generally temporary by definition. Change with purpose, though, is critical because when it comes to personal transformation, incremental change produces permanent results.

As humans, we certainly resist change, don't we? This aversion to change is normal. Change is uncomfortable. Often our aversion to change is driven by our past experience with a lack of genuine transformation. We see others "try" a diet and fail, or "try" to learn a new language and quit. And, often, there is the "I never did that before" mentality.

When a computer geek named Jeff Bezos looked for an outlet for his talents, he hit upon the idea of selling books online. There were two hurdles. First, he didn't particularly like books. But the big one was that—you guessed it—no one had ever done that before! Bezos's venture lost money for years as it steadily acquired market share to become what we know today as Amazon.

In your own life, can you imagine where you would be if your attitude to *everything* was, "I've never done *that* before!" You'd never rollerblade, water ski, ride a motorcycle, take an airplane trip, jump off a diving board, write a book, sing a song, or . . . heck, do *anything*. You would literally still be in diapers.

What's your fear of change? If you're like most people, it's the fear of the unknown. A fifty-year-old woman once said to me, "I'd like to go back to college, but by the time I graduate, I'll be fifty-four."

I asked, "Well, how old will you be in four years if you *don't* go to college?"

Her real fear wasn't time, but the unknown—the college setting for a middle-aged woman among so many young people. How would she fit in? Would she be accepted?

Admittedly, some people are more "change" averse than others. They equate change with risk. But those willing to change in order to *transform* are those most likely to reap fantastic rewards. Think of companies like Facebook, Google, Amazon.com, Fed-Ex and yes, Apple. They chose the route of risk for transformation sake. In doing so they didn't just change, but transformed the way we communicate, research information, read books, ship things, and make technology personal.

In fact, Apple was founded on the simple concept of "Think Differently." On the personal side, we must embrace the willingness to face our fear of change and the associated risk if we truly want to transform how we communicate. There are a million reasons why we would like to continue the way we've always communicated, but what if . . . what if you actually started to take the tools you've learned in this book and apply them on a regular basis?

"Everyone thinks of changing the world, but no one thinks of changing himself."
—Leo Tolstoy

Why Change is Necessary . . . and Difficult!

Change is a process. Incremental change is the first step toward transformation, and to become a transformed story-based communicator. To successfully transform people and an organization, you must—like a good artilleryman—soften up the ground before the assault. What then are the major obstacles to change that you must target? According to professional management expert Ken Blanchard, the process of change requires overcoming six obstacles.[21]

OBSTACLE TO CHANGE #1:
We feel awkward when we change.

That's because whenever you do anything new, you're bound to make mistakes. You can prepare people for change by knowing what they will experience, what they will expect, and to assure them (through example) that you made exactly the same mistakes learning the process.

Any new physical activity—whether playing table tennis or skateboarding or fly-fishing—takes practice. Ladies, why are so many men afraid of getting on a dance floor? Because it is awkward when they haven't had the practice to be good at it. (For some of you, when it comes to certain topics like dancing, transformation is out of reach—sorry. You know who you are.) Ever wonder why country line dancing caught on? Are there really that many people who like to wear cowboy boots? No, but country bars learned that they could get newcomers of both sexes to participate by offering line dancing classes. If everyone learns a new habit or practice at the same time, everyone will make similar mistakes and no one will feel, well, stupid.

Establish a setting that permits people to make mistakes without penalties. Encourage them to "go for it," and when they attempt something so difficult you know they will likely fail initially, provide them with a smaller, morale building task where they can succeed quickly and continue building.

While it is painful, sometimes people need to see for themselves the weakness of an idea or the folly of an approach. This can even have life and death implications. During the American Civil War, as General Ulysses S. Grant began his siege of the crucial Confederate stronghold of Vicksburg, his men grumbled about digging trenches and earthworks. They wanted to fight and decisively defeat the

Rebels rather than sit for weeks in the mud and starve their enemy out. Grant knew he did not have their confidence and they did not believe in his plan. He ordered a frontal attack—at a high cost. Hundreds of Union soldiers were killed or wounded in the attack, and men rapidly poured back into their trenches.

Without a speech, a chart, or even a single statement, Grant had demonstrated to every soldier the futility of a head-on assault. When they resumed digging their trenches, they were highly motivated, and willingly conducted the siege that eventually forced 11,000 Confederates to surrender with almost no further Union losses.

Your goal, of course, is to create a laboratory for experimenting with change while ensuring that you or your teammates don't do permanent damage to themselves or the company while they learn their lesson. Sales managers, in particular, need to remember it is important that your sales teams *learn*, not that you *teach* them. Allow them to flail around a bit. Let them learn from the process.

Remember the butterfly? It's only through struggling to get out of the cocoon that it strengthens its wings enough to fly. If you simply cut a hole in the cocoon to "let" the butterfly out, it will die. Interesting, huh? We must struggle through change at times to ensure true, complete transformation. Remember, very few people have ever said how beautiful a caterpillar or a cocoon is. Give yourself some time.

OBSTACLE TO CHANGE #2:
We feel alone.

At one point in our workshops, we pair people up to see how well they can recognize "change." In some cases, we've had as many as one hundred fifty different pairs going through the workshop in the same room at the same time. What's illuminating is how nearly everyone senses they are going through the exercise "alone" even though they are going through the exact same scenario as half the room, many of whom are only an arm's length away.

For most of us, we certainly look inward during change and begin to lose focus on our surroundings. We try our best to crawl back in our box, our safety zone. At work, many of you have been through sales force restructurings or organizational downsizing; it's easy to feel isolated during these times even though hundreds of others are experiencing the same thing. In our personal lives, those who have gone through a divorce or family hardship feel extremely isolated. What they don't realize is that many others are experiencing the same issues, probably even on their very own street.

It's instinctive to "hunker down" when change springs up, but it's not the best way to deal with it! Another big challenge we face when convincing others to try new things is a person's fear of standing out, of committing an embarrassing mistake alone in front of a crowd.

My pastor once told the story of a family that had the minister over for dinner. The table was beautifully set, mother and father and the three kids were at their assigned places, and everything was perfect for their guest. No sooner had the minister sat down than the youngest child, a seven-year-old girl, reached for her water goblet and knocked it over, spilling all over the table. For a moment the family sat there horrified, mother because her setting was ruined, the girl because she had just embarrassed everyone— until the minister smiled, looked over, and deliberately tipped his goblet over as well. Suddenly everyone laughed and each in turn tipped his or her own goblet over. What could have been a tense moment of extreme embarrassment for the girl became a shared experience in comedy.

Find a way to involve everyone in the process, letting him or her take turns at, well, looking foolish from time to time. Have you ever water-skied? How many times did it take you to get up the first time? If you were going to try to convince a friend to water ski, which would be the most likely to succeed—toss her out of a boat and hit the gas, or show some videos of yourself when you first flopped face first into the water . . . again, and again, and again?

If people know they are not alone in a process of change, they not only become more confident, but they become more willing to help others who are struggling as much as they are. Individual success becomes team success.

OBSTACLE TO CHANGE #3:
You fear you might have to give up something.

If your office converted from PCs to the Mac computers, you may experience a great deal of anxiety. Show others what they gain by adopting the new process, practice, or tool. People might lose the familiarity with saving or moving files, but gain faster processing and better review functions for their work.

One of our clients recently converted the entire sales force from laptops to tablets. The resistance was immense. We are creatures of habit, and for most of the employees the thought of "losing" the extra memory and perceived larger capacity terrified them. In the end, however, they found the tablet actually had better functionality to engage with their particular customers more effectively. It was easier to navigate and much more efficient to lug around all day!

Isn't it funny that in situations such as this, where resistance is futile, we still resist? We still feel like we're getting a raw deal, don't we. That's because we are focused on what we *might* be giving up, not what we could gaining. We all need to give our stories room to grow.

OBSTACLE TO CHANGE #4:
We can only take so much change at one time.

Any writer knows that the biggest impediment to writing is to start. Political commentator and fiction writer William F. Buckley, Jr. was once asked how he found time to write his weekly political column, a novel every year, and a non-fiction book every couple of years. He said, "I get up, I brush my teeth, and I sit down at the typewriter." While we've given up on typewriters, the order is still the same. Whatever your objective, you must set clear priorities with *incremental* goals that you can reach. My grandfather used to say, "Difficult things take a long time . . . the impossible just takes a little longer."

But when people get in the habit of doing difficult things, soon nothing seems impossible. On the other hand, if we try to take on too many things at once, we become overwhelmed and get nothing accomplished. The key is to prioritize the activities around change in an orderly, manageable fashion. You've heard the old adage, "How do you eat an elephant? One bite at a time!" This is true with change as well. Take it one small incremental step at a time. I don't personally recommend eating elephants anyway.

A friend has a son who plays video games online where heroes "level up" to gain new powers and abilities. The first level is always the easiest and comes the quickest, but then it gets steadily harder after that. Why? Because the game makers didn't want kids discouraged early, but found if they only incrementally increased the difficulty the kids would stay with it. This perfectly illustrates how you should approach change in your life. Set the "game" up so you can have early success and then build upon it incrementally until you've achieved transformation.

> "Difficult things take a long time; the impossible just takes a little longer."
> —WILLIE "PAPAW" BLOOMFIELD

OBSTACLE TO CHANGE #5:
We tend to always think we don't have enough resources.

There is nothing wrong with planning. The Bible instructs people to "count the cost" before they start building a house. Any family not over its head in debt has carefully looked at its family resources before buying a new car or a new house.

In business, managers must make sure they have the resources they need so they can't be blamed for failing to complete a job. Yet human nature is that we always want more, and think we "need" more. This is as true at your job as at home. Be creative. A professor friend of mine told me that while students may complain about the high cost of college, he presents to them four or five essay contests, paid internships, and scholarships worth sometimes thousands and even tens of thousands of dollars. He said, "In twenty-five years I've only had one student fill out the paperwork and seek the funds." He "got it." Sometimes the resources are on your doorstep, but because they don't come packaged in a familiar box, you don't see them.

The point is, as my grandpa used to say, "There's more than one way to skin a cat!" (I don't think PETA was around back then.) If you need resources, there are many ways to obtain them. Surround yourself with people who can acquire their own resources and who encourage your innovation. I believe this program is one of the key resources you will be able to add to your toolbox to help you achieve both your personal and professional goals.

OBSTACLE TO CHANGE #6:
Without pressure to change, we tend to stay the same.

This is one of those laws of the universe you learned in high school: that all life is governed by entropy, or the fact that all things head toward stasis. Hot things cool off; cool things heat up toward equilibrium. It is human nature too—this is back to Obstacle #1. If you don't think so, look at how easy it is for men to begin watching a football game upright in an easy chair. Before you know it, they are in a reclining position, asleep by halftime. In my experience this is the most common obstacle by far. In general, we have a tendency to try, fail, try harder, fail, and then revert back to our initial state and accept it as "good enough." The key is to keep yourself motivated to pursue the transformation you're after. Accountability peers, partners, coaches, and friends who can encourage you to stay on track are also excellent ways to reach your goal.

Yes, I know you have created a nice, comfortable, safe "box" in which you can quickly and easily retreat towards at the first sign of trouble. I'd like to challenge you to step outside of that box for just a bit and try something you've never tried before. In doing so, just know that you are not going through this alone. Many have started the first step in their Story-Based Selling journey and have found it to be transformative in their communication approach. It will seem a bit "clunky" for some of you at first. Resist the urge to jump back in your box!

These are the dynamics of change, and the obstacles we all encounter when we try to change anything, whether a process, a product, or behavior. Enough small changes and you will have a transformation—of your communication, your business, even your life. After you've finished this book, you'll have a tough decision to make. Should you continue down the path you've been on, or will you take a chance at something "different" that just may transform the way you communicate forever.

WHAT'S *YOUR* STORY?

✱ *What are the biggest changes you've ever had to go through?*

✱ *When you reflect on the "obstacles" to change, is there one that jumps out as your biggest struggle right now?*

✱ *How do you think your customers feel when they are asked to change?*

✱ *What can you do today to become a more positive "change agent" at your company? In your home?*

✱ *What in your life needs to go beyond "change" into full-blown "transformation?"*

.

8

Setting the Tone

"There is No Life I Know to Compare
with Pure Imagination."

—WILLY WONKA
Willy Wonka and the Chocolate Factory

Have you ever heard someone say, "Oh, I sure got him on the wrong day?" Have you ever talked to a client right before they got some bad news, or while they were trying to quit smoking and craving a cigarette? In a perfect world you are going to walk into every situation where the person making the decisions just got back from a golf trip and is still savoring his first hole in one, or found out her son just got a full-ride scholarship to Harvard.

Wouldn't it be great if that were always the setting? I think we all know that is not always the case. Okay, let's be honest, that is rarely the case. The fact is, very few stories are set in paradise. And even then, a popular story theme is, "trouble in paradise." Some of our greatest stories do not have the most ideal backdrops. *Slaughterhouse Five* is set in war torn Germany and *The Grapes of Wrath* in The Dust Bowl during The Great Depression. The point is simple; you are unlikely to get someone at his or her best.

"When trust improves, the mood improves."—FERNANDO FLORES

Author and humorist, Jon Acuff, once said, "Bridge the gap between your day job and your dream job." I appreciate this because, quite frankly, I enjoy what I do. But I also realize that many people

I encounter do not have the same philosophy. Countless people dread Monday mornings as much as they love Friday afternoons.

So let's say you have an appointment with someone on a loathsome Monday. You may be able to pick up quite early that they are not exactly on the sunny side of the street. Is all lost? Do you just chalk it up to *catching someone on a bad day?* I hope not. At this point in the book you should have a pretty good idea where I'm going with this. If you said, *tell a story,* pat yourself on the back.

Why is a story so important here? Well, maybe this guy dreads his job for a reason. Maybe he is so burned-out from balancing accounts and scrutinizing spreadsheets that he is numb to numbers. So if you come in and toss out facts and figures, you might as well just pile more dirt on what he has considered a very dead day. Remember the "Limbic Filter?" You have no idea what sort of junk this guy has in his brain trunk! No IT guy out there can defrag what you can with a story.

Start with a smile. And by smile, make it real. In business, a smile is just as important as a handshake. It should be a genuine smile, because you should enjoy what you do, even on Mondays. One of my daughter's close friends has one of those smiles that lights up a room. She is always a breath of fresh air at just the right time. Recently, her dad related a story where he asked her why she seemed to have this "thing" for going up to complete strangers who were not smiling and giving them her best smile. Her reply? "Dad, they looked sad, and I have plenty of smiles, so I thought I'd just give them one of mine."

Guess how many smiles she sees reflected back on any given day? You got it. This act of sharing a bit of yourself right from the start might be the only real smile your customer sees all day. There is something different about you; you don't look like you belong there. This is a good thing. If you do not start out by rattling off streams of left-brain information, they will relax a little, and be a bit of an easier audience. As mentioned previously, you want to reduce the level of anxiety for *both* of you.

Speaking of your audience, they certainly are not all easy. In fact, there are some tough rooms out there. A stand-up comedian lives and dies by his audience. Some nights, under the blinding stage lights, a comic feels like he is alone behind the microphone because there is no laughter coming from the seats. What he has to do is keep with the routine that had the previous night's crowd bellowing. There are tough nights on the stage, and there are tough days at work. Remember what you have rehearsed. It was good enough to get you this far, and it will get better. So will your attitude.

> "Those who dream by day are cognizant of many things that escape those who dream only at night."
> —EDGAR ALLEN POE
> "Eleonora"

People relate to "bad day" stories because I have yet to meet someone who has escaped them. Tell the person about the time you got a flat tire on the day you were already late for work, so to make up time you hit the accelerator a little harder than the police officer thought necessary, and this was sadly the highlight of your day because you soon discovered that you had forgotten your anniversary.

What happens next? Well, do not be too surprised if he tops you, and adds that he had a similar experience, only that his speeding ticket came in a school zone, and the police officer was his less-than-proud father-in-law.

You are not patronizing him by laughing, because that stuff is funny. We all have had that day where if something could go wrong, it did. But a bad day is exactly that—a bad *day*. It has an expiration, and do not let it carry to the next day. I'll bet most of you know people who do not say they are having a bad day; he or she feels like they are having a bad life. How enjoyable are those people? How much do you want to be like them?

Let's go back to the active listening exercises. If you are talking with someone who is complaining, do you hear more than complaints? Chances are the person is communicating more than just endless gripes. His problem here is that he may have put himself in a position where people no longer hear what he is saying. You can make yourself different just by listening to what he is really saying. It is probably more than just complaints.

Do you need to change your story? Where do you start? Your first thought may be to say that the setting needs to change. I question this line of thinking because misery can travel along with you. That's why they call it baggage.

But what's another key component of a story? Well, don't forget mood. *Webster's Dictionary* defines a mood as: a prevailing attitude; a receptive state of mind predisposing to action; or a distinctive atmosphere or context. How prevalent is mood in the case of the guy loathing everything around him on Monday morning? Think back to chapter two where we discussed "neural coupling." Neural coupling is the process where people began to unconsciously imitate one another. There is something truly powerful in place here. You have the ability to shine light in the dark. It's all part of the brain's subconscious "mirroring" neurons. When you smile, they smile back. When you yawn, it creates a chain reaction. Being positive can create a domino like effect of positivity.

This whole concept is simple enough, but why is there still such difficulty? Are your thoughts and feelings not on the same page, creating some sort of discord? Is it still uncomfortable to share your story?

You'll remember we talked earlier about Dr. Mehrabian's discovery around the three elements of communication—words, tone, and body language. They are listed in that order for a reason, easiest to hardest. It is relatively easy to put the words of a story together. All you have to do is take the time to write them down, since they are already swimming around in your head.

**"Body language is a very powerful tool.
We had body language before we had speech."**
—DEBORAH BULL, dancer with The Royal Ballet, author of *Dancing Away*

But what happens the first time you read it? How natural does it sound? You may find yourself tripping over the words you just wrote down. The words are not comfortable right away. It takes time for something to flow naturally from the page to your mouth. If you read some beautiful writing, like Psalm 23 or a Shakespearian sonnet, but if you do so in an uninterested, monotone voice, how engaging is it? Give the words life. Give your story a voice. Give it *your* voice!

Now in your best infomercial voice say, "But wait, there's more!" The way you carry yourself is very important, and the final part of Dr. Mahrabian's equation. Up until this point you may have everything in place, but are you creating separation with your customer? Do you *look* uncomfortable and fidgety? Do you keep looking at your watch or at a sales invoice?

Your customer will pick up on this and not trust you. The solution here is not complicated, but not necessarily easy either. If you want your customer to trust you, you have to trust yourself. Practice your story, know your story, and along the way you will discover things about yourself as well.

The creative process does belong in the workplace, not just when someone tries to motivate you by saying, "Think outside the box." Personally, I could not imagine a day where I did not use the creative process. Do not check your right brain at the door when your workday starts.

How do you feel when you read your favorite book or hear your favorite song? Chances are it is far different than the Monday morning doldrums. How do you escape that feeling? First, you have to escape yourself. I am pretty certain that God did not create any of us to be miserable. We are created to be relational.

Stories are transformative. Narnia and Oz may be fictitious, but while you are reading the pages or watching the screen, why does it feel so real? If you ever want to get on my bad side, remind me that Luke Skywalker did not really live *long ago, in a galaxy far, far away.*

There is enough power in childhood imagination to believe that you can climb through an old wardrobe, and end up in a magical land. Even if Dorothy was on a yellow brick road with a scarecrow, tin man, and lion, we all related to going on a journey trying to find the way home. And who never dreamed of leaving a pedestrian life to be a hero and find your real calling?

We relate to Luke Skywalker because he felt stuck on Tattoine, where nothing was ever going to happen. Many of us have our own Tattoine, which we call a cubicle, an office or for most of you in sales, your car.

Now let's go back to the guy fighting the great beast called Monday. Does he feel like he's preparing to blow up the Death Star and save the galaxy, or is he so defeated that he will not even dare to dream any longer? You have shared your story, and he has shared some of his. Do you think any of this would happen if you started in with the facts and figures? You have made some connection with a tough crowd, and that's like the comedian who is dying on stage finally getting a chuckle. You have to start somewhere, and stories, like laughter, grow. Ask him a little more about his story. Don't you like it when people take a genuine interest in you? Since we all have stories to tell, we want that story to be told.

His story may be funny, sad, or inspirational, but what you will receive is something genuine. It takes vulnerability to be genuine. It is also refreshing, and you have done nothing but scratch the surface. But in doing so, you may find an actual person hiding beneath that frown. Does he see you as a salesperson, or a superhero who just slayed that vicious dragon called Monday?

Okay, that may have been a bit of a stretch, but you did win a battle. The pen is certainly mightier than the sword when battling a beast like misery. And to throw out another old expression, remember "Misery Loves Company"? You did not share in his misery; instead you shared a miserable experience and were able to laugh about it. It did not beat you. He will not say this, but he noticed it. He saw a little of your story, and would listen to more. And he's probably ready to tell more of his.

He was probably all too ready to tell you no when you first walked in that door. You were just a salesperson, and certainly not the first he has ever encountered. You were just facts and figures, and he was a rebuttal waiting to happen. It was the same old song and dance.

Remember that stories, like humans, are relational. What did Tom Hanks do in *Castaway* when he was lonely? He made a friend. From the very first human, it was decided that it is not good to be alone. So out on the desert island, with nobody around and nobody looking for him, he created Wilson, who was a decorated volleyball.

Was Wilson real? Does it matter? In fact, I will even argue that in this movie, Wilson saved Tom Hanks' life. Really. If he had nobody, he would have given up. His fiancée thought he was dead and the world had moved on without him. He talked to Wilson, and he even had room for him on his escape raft. After all, it promised to be a long and dangerous journey. He needed that support. When he crafted Wilson the mood of the story began to transition from sorrow to hope. Connections can do that, even if it is an inanimate object.

I would like to think most of you have better friends than volley-balls, but this is a strong image of how powerful the imagination can be. You have had this all along, but let me reinforce it. It's the power of imagination. It's where all stories live. It's where all ideas are created, both big and small.

"I saw the angel in the marble and carved until I set him free."
—MICHELANGELO, *Lettera a messer Benedtto Varchi*

I was washing some plates a while ago, and I dropped the dish-towel. I never got the dishtowel back. That's because it was no lon-ger a dishtowel. It transformed as soon as a five-year-old swooped in and picked it up, put it around his neck, and started running with his arms extended. Yes, all of a sudden my dishtowel was a cape and my son, Drew was flying around the living room.

I found an empty tube of wrapping paper by the wastebasket, picked it up and chased him. We both knew full well that it was never a paper roll—it was always a sword. I chased him, but do you know how hard it is to catch a kid with super powers? What is this great power that we possess in abundance as children, yet seems to fade as we age? Imagination! He was wrapped up in hero mode, and I could not have stopped him if I wanted to.

Of course I didn't want to. He rescued me that day. I was sticking to my script of washing the dishes, but he had a better idea. Actually, he had a lot of ideas, which included slaying dragons and chasing bank robbers. Like any child, he effortlessly made it all up as he went. The scenes changed and the plot thickened until he decided it was time for a snack. Saving the planet is hard work, and can really work up the appetite.

The dishes eventually got washed. Unfortunately there were no super powers that let me finish them in a snap, but they did get washed. I could scratch that off my transactional list of things that needed done. But something else happened. I went away from my script, and was greatly rewarded for it. I also wondered when that dishtowel stopped being a cape and when the tube was no longer a sword.

That's what I want to give back to you. While I am not suggesting you show up at the office with a dishtowel wrapped around your neck, not even on casual Friday, but you are not doing yourself any favors by dismissing childlike imagination. You can also change the script.

Ask any author if their final draft ended up exactly the way they envisioned. Ideas pop up along the way; characters end up doing things that even the writer never expected. When the story really starts getting going, the author is only the first viewer of the action.

Sounds absurd, doesn't it? This is not logical, and what it doesn't understand unsettles the left brain. If you have a script, why go off it? It is there to get you to where you need. Legendary musician, John Lennon famously wrote, "Life is what happens while you're making other plans."

I know an author who had an idea for a novel. He created characters that felt real to him, and the story was very personal. The way he envisioned this story, however, involved the lead character dying at the end. It seemed to make perfect sense and worked in the perceived arc of the plot. As the story unfolded, he felt like he knew him like a brother and would mourn him when he eventually died. He still considered this to be a good thing and hoped his readers would have the same connection.

A funny thing happened on the way to total destruction. He discovered that his character was way stronger than he ever believed. The author realized that he had written an ending with redemption and hope. The left brain would have killed this character because it was a more logical conclusion. The right brain handled the problem-solving through insight.

It is good to have a plan, do not get me wrong here, but no road map is perfect. You will always face detours and hazards. You will probably think, but that's not in the plan! What happens next? Your right brain is well equipped to make adjustments and will probably find a much more scenic route.

Have you ever listened to someone who basically sounds like a robot? They have rehearsed their script so thoroughly it no longer has life to them. How engaged are they with you? Do you feel any connection? Imagine this like a movie that was written by the right brain, but is directed by the left. The correct words are spoken, but they are flat and formulaic. Is that how you want your story to sound?

Earlier we talked about traits of great communicators. Remember the enthusiasm? Remember the consistency? You may not be playing Carnegie Hall, but you are on a stage, and you have an audience.

We also talked about having a few stories. And since it is your story, tell it the way that feels best in the right situation. You know the details; after all, you've lived them. If you sense that you are getting a response when you tell the part of your story involving your kids, expand upon that. The left brain will not understand, since it was not part of the initial plan, but the intuition in the right brain has this handled. As you pick up on these clues, you are connecting with your customer. In doing so, you are also opening up for them to share their story. When they share their story, they are engaging with you. When they engage with you, trust is established.

While I was washing the dishes, if I had been in left-brain mode, I would have continued with my script of methodically cleaning the plate, but only after retrieving the dishtowel. The dishtowel was a necessary tool to complete the task. My right brain allowed me to see what my son was able to see. Sure, the left brain may have argued that this was just a ploy to get out of a tedious job, but it was more than that. Putting off doing the dishes for a while was just an added benefit. I will allow that concession.

So when you look at your story, are you giving it the freedom it needs to grow? Are you giving it the life it needs to be relatable? Is it still exciting to you?

WHAT'S *YOUR* STORY?

* *Do you "count your losses" or try to change the mood in a room?*

* *Do you get frustrated when things do not go according to plan?*

* *Are you comfortable enough to adapt your story?*

* *Do you find your customers beginning to share their own stories?*

* *Do you see imagination as something experienced in childhood or something to practice daily?*

9

Time to Tell Your Story

"There is Nobody Youer Than You"

—Dr. Seuss

It may not seem like we spent a whole lot of time talking about sales in what you thought was going to be a book designed to help your productivity. You have likely never thought about neuroscience and the elements of a story when you did your day job before. Whether your reason for picking this book up was as simple as an attempt to boost your commissions, or if you genuinely found the opportunity to transform your communication intriguing, I hope you now realize you can have both.

My goal for you is that a journey through Story-Based Selling will help you overcome the communication obstacles you currently face and will face everyday on the sales battlefield.

The simple truth here is that the brain is an incredibly complex organ, particularly when it comes to communication. The right brain and left brain are not always the best neighbors to each other, and the subconscious mind drives us a whole lot further than we tend to give it credit for. Along the winding way there can be misunderstanding and/or mistrust, and we all know that both never lead to anything good. No wonder so many live with such disconnect. No wonder there is such difficulty with communication.

Decades ago, I first learned of the famous Plot Diagram in Mr. Diebler's fifth grade class.

```
                    /\
                   /  \
                  /    \
                 /      \
        RISING  /        \
        ACTION /          \
              /            \
             /    FALLING   \
            /     ACTION     \
    _____/                  _____
    EXPOSITION              RESOLUTION
```

Who can forget the framework of introduction, rising action, climax, falling action (or dénouement if you wanted extra credit), and conclusion? At that time, I thought all I would need to do is pass that test, and never look back at it again. Who would have thought I would use it in a sales career?

In the movie *Dead Poets Society*, Robin Williams emphasized for his class of left-brained thinkers to "Make your lives extraordinary." Early in the film, he asked them what "Carpe Diem" meant. While they could easily translate the words ("Seize the day"), there was much greater difficulty with living it out.

Why? Don't we all want our lives to be amazing? What is holding us back? There was also a point in the movie where he had the students read a section from a poetry book. This book suggested that you could quantify the value of a story by prescribing a mathematical formula. Some of the students nodded in absent agreement, but were then totally thrown awry when he told them to rip that out of their books and throw it away.

That's exactly what I want you to do right now. Rip sections out of your own "book" and throw them away. Here are a few examples that need to be tossed:

The Myth That Emotional Connections Aren't Important

Many of us (especially men) were raised in environments where showing emotion or vulnerability was a sign of weakness. It's one thing to break down crying at every long-distance phone commercial, but throwing the proverbial emotional baby out with the bathwater is a big mistake. By no means do I feel that every one of us needs to crawl up on Dr. Phil's comfy couch on a daily basis, but I do believe many of us resist opportunities to emotionally connect with others because of the myriad of junk in our brain trunks. We may be conditioned to keep our emotions close to our vest, but as you can clearly see now, the brain is a complex animal and it's going to think on it's own anyway.

By resisting the emotional connection or any chance to even attempt this connection, you are sending subconscious signals to the other person that you are not *truly* interested in them. In sales, this is a deal killer. In life, this is a relationship killer. It wreaks havoc on marriages, friendships, and parent to child relationships. By being open to these emotions, you actually demonstrate more credibility and strength. It may not feel that way today, but the more you let go and try, the easier it will be. And the more you will feel connected to others as well.

The Myth That Visualized Goals Cannot Be Reality

In this context, let's call the goal *pre-reality*. If you don't believe something before it happens, then it never will. Visualize where you see yourself going. (Guess which side of the brain you'll be using?)

There are few things more mechanical than a golf swing. The entire body must be working in perfect harmony to hit a small ball straight. Now if you have ever played a round, even if you don't have an instructor on the course, chances are there is someone behind you telling you what you are doing wrong. Either your backswing is too fast, you've opened up a shoulder, or you don't keep your head down. Any of those things can make for a long day.

Now I don't have a whole lot of bragging rights on the course, but I do remember the first time I hit a shot, and was able to just watch it without wanting to throw my club into the lake. I had an instructor who told me what to do, but before I even stepped into the tee box, he told me to visualize hitting a great shot.

So I did. I believed I was going to hit it deep into the fairway and I was then watching it happen. I saw the shot in my mind so vividly. I owned it. The old expression about possession being nine-tenths of the law rang true.

Be positive and expect good things. When they happen, you will know what to do with them.

The Myth That There Are No Happy Endings

Negativity breeds more negativity. So many people work so hard to avoid disappointment that they sabotage good things before they can happen. Yes, sometimes hopes and dreams do end in disappointment. That is part of life, but don't let that be the only part of your life.

I worked with a guy who was really hoping for a promotion. He had the right qualifications, but perhaps not the right attitude. He kept saying, "Oh, they'll probably give it to someone else."

He was worried about being disappointed, so he prepared himself for it. He was prepared to say, "See? I was right." He certainly was not prepared for a new opportunity. Needless to say, his story was filled with negativity, and as such, not very engaging. And guess what? He didn't get the job. If you struggle with negativity, try changing your position. Sometimes a change in position is all you need to change your perspective. By position, it could literally be your job but more than likely, it's just a metaphor for how you currently view life or some aspect of your life.

The Myth That Stories Don't Require Preparation

So how do you tell your story? Well, you know it, but how well do you know it?

Before you stand in front of a crowd, or even another person, work it out. Maybe even write it down. You may be a little surprised by what you read on the page. You know that brain thing we talked about, well, it is a powerful source, and you can tap into it with a pen. Many authors do not sit in front of their computer just because they have a story to tell; Instead they want to see what they truly had, and pardon the pun, *in mind.*

You also do not need to be Charles Dickens to write. Legendary basketball coach Bobby Knight once said, when annoyed with reporters, "All of us learn to write in the second grade. Most of us go on to greater things."

Okay, this quote is a bit harsh, but it states that there is not a special skill set involved. It requires discipline and honesty, and that is the basis for any successful platform.

And now for a few things to add to your "to do" list . . .

Listen to Yourself

Read your words like an objective reader would. Yes, you wrote the words, but before you start to mark them up with a red pen, look for the essence, look for the passion. Have you ever listened to someone who was entirely too polished? Sure they may have seemed like a great speaker, but did you connect with them? If not, perhaps they weren't so great after all. Become your own best coach. Record your stories on your smart phone and play them back. Be objective. Don't stop improving.

Tell Stories Fearlessly

The biggest mistake we make in storytelling is not engaging in the process for fear of making a mistake. It really comes down to being comfortable in your own storytelling "skin." You have so much ammunition at your disposal. I have yet to meet another human being who doesn't have wonderful, powerful, and engaging stories to tell. They sometimes just don't realize it. Start small with a few "go to" stories and build your repertoire over time. Don't be afraid of looking foolish. Heck, most of my stories are about times when I felt like an idiot trying to tell a story! No one will remember that you screwed up your story. They will remember how you reacted to it with humility and how they "felt" connected to you anyway.

Have Fun

Let's be honest, if you are not going to have fun with telling stories, you might as well just go back to spouting off facts and figures. But remember, if you keep doing what you've always done, don't complain when you keep getting what you've always gotten. Telling your story should be a great experience, so do not hinder yourself with any more excuses. Laugh at the funny stuff and cry at the sad. Shudder with the horror and embrace the love.

Share

Start practicing, even if you are not comfortable with it yet. Many of us battle the myth of perfection. We feel like we must have something perfect before it can be shared. Let me be clear on this, you are never going to get there. And even if you do somehow reach this inhuman level, chances are you will still feel like there is some part of it that still needs work.

Great and shared is infinitely better than perfect and left alone. And even if you were perfect, how many people would relate to you?

Be Yourself

This is something I can't do for you. This is something nobody can do for you. But sadly, this is something that most people don't do for themselves. We are created with a story unfolding within us on a daily basis. Catch that story, set it free and see what comes back to you.

WHAT'S *YOUR* STORY?

❀ *How are you trying to make your life extraordinary?*

❀ *Are you held up by the myth of perfection?*

❀ *Do you edit your story before you get to the good stuff?*

❀ *Think about a story that truly resonated with you. What part do you remember the most?*

❀ *Are you optimistic or do you disengage because you work too hard to avoid disappointment?*

Afterword

Okay, we're not done just yet. That's because I want to hear *your* story. I learned to tell stories by listening to them first, and this part of my job never gets old. So therefore I want you to share your story with me, and all of us on our training team.

Vision is not a goal to be accomplished, rather a passion to be pursued.

Keep in contact with us; we can help you move from being stuck to soaring. It's what we do, and I love my job.

jeff@jeffbloomfield.com
www.jeffbloomfield.com
or
www.braintrust101.com

Endnotes

1   Luke 10:33, *New King James Bible*.

2   Stephen R. Covey. "The Leader Formula: The 4 Things That Make a Good Leader" http://www.stephencovey.com/blog/.

3   "The Top 10 Best and Worst Communicators of 2011," http://www.prdaily.com/Main/Articles/The_top_10_best_and_worst_communicators_of_2011__10321.aspx.

4   Oprah Winfrey. Commencement Speech at Howard University, 2007, http://www.graduationwisdom.com/speeches/0024-winfrey.htm.

5   Billy Graham. "Celebrating Our Freedoms," July 4, 1970.

6   www.mylifeinministry.com/characteristics-of-a-great-communicator.

7   www.london.edu/facultyandresearch.html.

8   Greg J. Stephens, Lauren J. Silbert, and Uri Hasson. "Speaker–Listener Neural Coupling Underlies Successful Communication" (Proc Natl Acad Sci USA, August 10, 2010).

9   World Bank. (n.d.). The learning pyramid worldbank.org/DEVMARKETPLACE/Resources/Handout_The-LearningPyramid.pdf.

10   http://storytellingquotes.tumblr.com/post/7842615111.

11   http://www.fastcoexist.com/1678486.

12   http://www.amazon.com/Whole-New-Mind-Right-Brainers-Future/dp/1594481717.

13   http://steam-notstem.com/about/whitepaper/.

14   "How My Predictions are Fairing," Ray Kurzweil, Oct. 2010.

15   Richard Maxwell and Robert Dickman. *The Elements of Persuasion: Use Storytelling to Pitch Better, Sell Faster & Win More Business* (New York: Harper Business, 2007), p125.

16   Jenni Laidman. "Making an Impression," *Toledo Blade*, June 25, 2001.

17   Eliot R. Smith and Diane M. Mackie. *Social Psychology* (Oxford: Psychology Press, 2007), 57, 86.

18   Franklin Institute, "Attack of the Adrenals: A Metabolic Story," http://www.fi.edu/learn/brain/stress.html.

19   http://futureofstorytelling.org/video/empathy-neurochemistry-and-the-dramatic-arc/

20   Abraham Lincoln. Speech in Springfield Illinois, June 16, 1848, http://showcase.netins.net/web/creative/lincoln/speeches/house.htm.

21   Ken Blanchard. "Understanding the Dynamics of Change," Professional Convention Management Association, http://pcma.org/Convene/Issue-Archives/May-1996/Under-standing-the-Dynamics-of-Change.htm.

About the Author

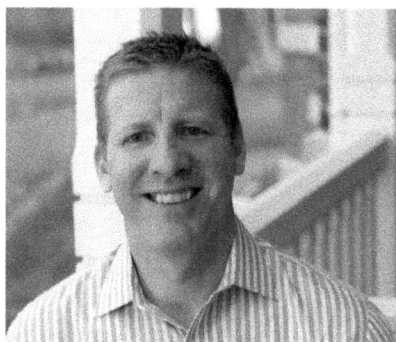

Jeff comes from a long line of storytellers. He has helped individuals and companies transform their sales and marketing systems by understanding the power of neuroscience on everyday communication.

Jeff has founded and managed two separated consulting companies, Apex Training & Development and most recently, Brain Trust. His dynamic, engaging, communication style, and his sense of humor and inspiring transformational coaching techniques are the trademark of his companies. His experience of over fifteen years in sales, marketing, and training in multiple industries affords him a unique perspective that seems to resonate with readers and clients of all backgrounds and industries.

From his former life as a senior manager at a world-wide leading bio-tech company through his varying roles in sales, marketing, and leadership development, Jeff's experience affords him the ability to partner with business owners and senior level executives from a perspective that truly understands their unique challenges in today's complex business environment. In addition, Jeff has his ICF Executive Coaching Certification through the Center for Executive Coaching.

Jeff resides in the Cincinnati, Ohio, area with his wife, Hazel, and two kids, Gracie and Drew. He is active in his community and church as well as international ministries to support orphans and the underprivileged.

www.ingramcontent.com/pod-product-compliance
Lightning Source LLC
Chambersburg PA
CBHW050501190326
41458CB00005B/1386